Imaginary Performances in Shakespeare

In *Imaginary Performances in Shakespeare*, visionary modernist theatre director Aureliu Manea analyses the theatrical possibilities of Shakespeare. Through nineteen Shakespeare plays, Manea sketches the intellectual parameters, the visual languages, and the emotional worlds of imagined stage interpretations of each; these nineteen short essays are appended by his essay 'Confessions,' an autobiographical meditation on the nature of theatre and the role of the director. This captivating book which will be attractive to anyone interested in Shakespeare and modern theatre.

Aureliu Manea made his debut as a director with a production of Ibsen's *Rosmersholm* at the Sibiu Theatre, which stunned Romania's theatrical world with the originality of its staging, and the press hailed him as a unique new talent. Throughout his career, he created a large number of theatre and opera productions, as well as puppet shows, creating a repertoire of both Romanian and foreign plays, some of which had never before been performed in Romania, such as Sophocles's *Philoctetes*. Manea is considered a Romanian director who revolutionised and reformulated theatre.

Imaginary Performances in Shakespeare

Aureliu Manea

Translated from the Romanian by Alistair Ian Blyth

First published as Spectacole imaginare, *Editura Dacia, Cluj, 1986*
Second edition, revised and expanded, Editura Eikon, Bucharest, 2018

LONDON AND NEW YORK

First published in English 2020
by Routledge
2 Park Square, Milton Park, Abingdon, Oxon OX14 4RN

and by Routledge
52 Vanderbilt Avenue, New York, NY 10017

Routledge is an imprint of the Taylor & Francis Group, an informa business

Translated by Alistair Ian Blyth

Published in Romanian first edition by Editura Dacia 1986, second edition
by EIKON 2018

British Library Cataloguing-in-Publication Data
A catalogue record for this book is available from the British Library

Library of Congress Cataloging-in-Publication Data
A catalog record for this book has been requested

ISBN: 978-0-36749-874-0

Typeset in Times New Roman
by Apex CoVantage, LLC

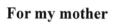

For my mother

Aureliu Manea (1945–2014)

Contents

Foreword

The production of *Twelfth Night* that my brother, Aureliu Manea, directed in Cluj in 1975 was the first time in my life that I witnessed a standing ovation. The final curtain had come down, but on stage, the music—the food of love—played on, and the audience simply refused to leave the auditorium. It was during the communist regime, and in the theatre in those days, the same as in literature and the arts in general, it was very hard to get past the censors, but my brother had always managed to sneak in a subtle and innocent message and audiences loved him for it.

He directed popularly and critically acclaimed productions of plays in Turda, a small city in Transylvania, and also in Ploieşti, Sibiu, Timişoara, Jassy, and other cities around Romania. Those plays included *Macbeth*, *Arden of Faversham*, Sophocles's *Philoctetes*, Seneca's *Medea*, Racine's *Phèdre* and *Britannicus*, Chekhov's *The Seagull* and *Three Sisters*, and Büchner's *Woyzeck*, as well as classics by Romanian playwrights Ion Luca Caragiale and Tudor Muşatescu, all of which earned him a reputation as an uncompromising, visionary director. But he staged only a single production in the capital, Bucharest, because he said that the actors there were too big. He worked better with lesser-known actors, who followed his directions without objection and displays of ego. He used to say that a play was not for the benefit of the actors, but an entity unto itself, and a theatrical performance was an act of love, of communion, that revealed the timeless dramatic text. For him, theatre transcended the individual, it possessed "infinite powers," it was the "art of human solidarity." He saw the performance of a play as almost mystical, a ritual of togetherness that united both actors and audience, like a musical harmony.

Imaginary Performances was published in Romania in 1986. It was a book born of love: my brother's love of people, the theatre, and, above all, Shakespeare, in whose works love of the human and the theatre together find their profoundest expression. He was always conscious of the paradox that the theatre is both transcendent and ephemeral, and those who at the time recognised his unique, innovative talent encouraged him to leave a permanent record of his vision, which took the form of these directorial meditations on the theatrical essence of nineteen of Shakespeare's plays and a series of deeply personal confessions on directing and acting that reveal his generosity of spirit and deep humanism. Unfortunately, there exist very few photographs of my brother's theatrical productions from the 1970s and 1980s, and there are no film recordings, but in this book his singular vision as a director lives on, and as a true believer in the universality of Theatre, he would have been moved to know that with this English translation his words will now travel beyond Romania to reach an international audience.

Viorica Samson

With its rich native traditions of dramatic metaphor and realist acting alike, and its long simultaneous engagement with both the French avant-garde and with Russian naturalism, the twentieth-century Romanian theatre provided the Shakespeare canon with one of its most productive latterday homes. A profound engagement with Shakespeare that had begun in the years when Romania was establishing itself as an independent European country rather than a fief of the Ottoman empire survived into a post-war political world of Soviet-style censorship, and while some directors, such as Liviu Ciulei and Radu Penciulescu, defected to the West, others stayed, pushing the limits of what could be said and thought in their explorations of this one playwright whom the regime could not be seen to ban. Under the tyranny of Ceauşescu, the Romanian theatre became a laboratory in which directors such as Aureliu Manea and Alexandru Tocilescu could still find in Shakespeare a supreme exemplar of freedom of expression. For theatregoers from farther West, the fact that ill health forced Aureliu Manea to retire from directing just after the collapse of Ceauşescu's regime, just as Romanian productions of Shakespeare were able both to tour abroad and to be seen and marvelled at by a wider range of overseas spectators, must remain a cause of lasting regret. It is a matter for rejoicing that thanks to the efforts of his sister, his writings on Shakespeare, the fruits of both real and imaginary productions, are now available to Anglophone readers for the first time.

Professor Michael Dobson

Part one
Imaginary performances

1 *Richard II*, or the revelation of failure

I think that before reading this text so full of enigmas and poetic beauty, the reader or the director called to stage it should consult Seneca's *Ad Lucilium Epistulae Morales*. In the first letter, the Roman philosopher says: "You will find that the largest portion of our life passes while we are doing ill, a goodly share while we are doing nothing, and the whole while we are doing that which is not to the purpose" (trans. Richard M. Gummere).

The whole of Shakespeare's play foregrounds a process of reaching awareness. In what is a kind of moral fable, the author tells us of that which is frail and defenceless in a man who falls down the social ladder. What we may be sure of is that in *Richard II* we are dealing with an archetype.

The fall from power of the young King Richard II provides us with an occasion to think deeply about sudden contact with the abyss. Misfortune wrenches from its victim the deepest cogitations. A quite obscure French philosopher once wrote that social failure cannot help but serve as a source of wisdom, since it brings awareness of one's limits. Once toppled, the young king, now a man like any other, measures himself against his peers. And what does Richard discover? What does the young Richard, if we may name him thus, discover once he no longer holds power? Let us listen to what he says:

> Cover your heads and mock not flesh and blood
> With solemn reverence: throw away respect,
> Tradition form and ceremonious duty,
> For you have but mistook me all this while:
> I live with bread like you, feel want,
> Taste grief, need friends: subjected thus,
> How can you say to me, I am a king?

This surprise, or even astonishment at things without consistency or durability, inspires the deposed young king to meditate on and try to understand man's higher purposes. What seems to me dramatic and paradoxical is that not even in the moment of death does poor Richard believe that power can be lost so easily. Through him, what comes crashing down is in fact the sacred right of kings. Bolingbroke is a vassal, a royal servant, but not a prince with sovereign rights. With fateful refinement, what Shakespeare conveys through this tragedy is the collapse of an entire world.

Since kingship belongs to the realm of immutable laws, the author suggests that the toppling of Richard II is sacrilegious. I have thought for a long time about the strange, enigmatic figure that is Richard. I imagine him as a young man rather like the character Thomas Mann describes in his novella *Tonio Kröger*. A tall, thin, blond, blue-eyed young man. Nature endowed him with precious gifts at birth, making him the epitome of human excellence. In order to draw a comparison with what happens to Richard, a comparison with regard to his deposed condition, I would suggest the moment when a child loses its parent in a crowd. Whoever has witnessed such a scene, which to some will seem commonplace, will recall the terrible fear that drives the child to tears. Such an existential situation might translate the feeling of the dethroned king.

There is nobody in the world who can protect him in this his hardest moment. His loneliness, the fear that stalks him, his vulnerability, the curses and injustices visited upon him all combine to enact a second coronation, the coronation of *failure*. In such a moment, youth swiftly ages and thoughts become profound.

I ask myself with whom we should side in such a confrontation? Shakespeare understands the toppled man, he suffers with him, but he cannot remain by his side. The juggernaut of history is more powerful than any species of feeling. In the face of the armies that support Bolingbroke, words are superfluous.

I would like to produce a performance in the form of a Nordic fairy tale about an unhappy prince. In my production, the sets would be suggestive of a meadow full of flowers. The setting would be a melancholy springtime. On the stage, sloping in Elizabethan style, I would ask the set designer to create a richly woven carpet to embody the grass and the wildflowers. Lost, bewildered, dressed in white, a frail young king wanders back and forth over this meadow, as if in search of something. The courtiers that accompany him are dressed in the most elegant of costumes, of the kind painted by the Renaissance masters.

In contrast, Bolingbroke's men, armed to the teeth, wear furs and scuffed leathers; they carry rusty shields. They cannot comprehend sickly refinement. In one corner of the stage, I see a shady bower of flowering trees. It is here that Richard will deliver his great soliloquies. Toward the end of the play, the prince's clothes will be tattered. He is tired, there are dark rings under his eyes, and his beard is unkempt. What more can be done for him? Nothing. Fate has proven merciless to him.

I think that *Richard II* is one of Shakespeare's most beautiful plays. The theme of my production will be human frailty. In fact, in the very first scene, one of the characters gives a Pascalian definition of man: "Men are but gilded loam or painted clay." It is precisely from this point of view that the whole dramatic structure must be analysed. An old world is collapsing, and it is shown no mercy. Those who are to come to power bring with them a rude health that can endure the cold. Richard II passes among them, surrounded by musicians. This will be the essential image of the performance. I see the young king accompanied everywhere by musicians. And as Shakespeare describes him, even in prison Richard hears a strange music, played in his honour.

What more can Richard do than die? For, as Martin Heidegger says, "Man alone dies and does so ceaselessly." We will be spiritually shaken by his fate and we will recognise the moral of this strange fable, hidden between its lines, namely that nothing human is eternal. All the things of the world in which we live are transient. And every mistake is punished mercilessly. The young king's mistake was to have lived life at the aesthetic level. He sampled all with splendid insouciance. He sucked the nectar of life from the corollas of the Great Garden. But he never thought of the future. How might we help him? We cannot. Mistakes must be paid for dearly. A gardener who appears at one point says:

> O, what pity is it
> That he had not so trimmed and dressed his land
> As we this garden!

The young king drags behind him a long train of political mistakes. I think about staging the production in a real garden. Like Adam, Richard tastes of the fruit of the Tree of Knowledge. His sin justifies nothing apart from an incomprehensible fear. Relying on his divine right, without consolidating his human relations, Richard will have to leave this wonderful garden, taking a journey of no return, a journey to an unmarked grave. Fate gazes on him with hideous visage. Thus, we trace a history in which awareness is regained. Formerly an unaware king, our character becomes an ordinary man, but thereby gains the gift of being able to philosophise. Toward the end, looking in the mirror, Richard says:

> A brittle glory shineth in this face:
> As brittle as the glory is the face.

I think that if the mere mortal named Richard were allowed to continue his life somewhere far away, as he himself demands, he would choose a way of life like that of Montaigne. Let us recognise that failure has made him wise! I am convinced that in his isolation he would have meditated on things eternal. Richard II is villainously slain. Nobody rejoices at his death. Not even the fortunate Bolingbroke. Richard's death casts a shadow of sadness over our souls. Those who have come to power are stern and austere. The luxury with which Richard surrounded himself has faded. His wife will flee to France.

I have been thinking about this play for a long time, but its enigma remains enveloped in a silvery mist. Poetic regret echoes from Shakespeare's text. I might also create a production set in the late nineteenth century, full of Proustian lyricism. An aristocratic world finds itself in a historical waste-land. The beautiful gesture for its own sake is no longer valued. It is no longer sought because it is no longer effective. A tenacious positivism urges vassals to take fate into their own hands. Desperate times are fast approaching. Around Richard, pomp and luxury distort life, and the young shoot has sickened.

Wars gather threateningly at the gates of the world, knocking to enter. What can Richard's fate mean to us? In Richard's case we are dealing with a human, so-called return to the self, in accordance with Pascal's theory. Richard has lived his life nonchalantly, and around him this nonchalance has created a cruel, oppressive, bewildering void. Rediscovering himself through *failure*, Richard discovers human wretchedness. The weaknesses of man in general are conceived as his own weaknesses. It is this that draws Richard closer to our hearts.

I picture the set of the production as a vast structure made up of books. The books are shrouded in a grey, silken veil. At the end, when he is close to death, Richard discovers the books. Ignored, unassuming, the books are at his disposal. Which book will Richard choose before he dies? Perhaps Montaigne's *Essays*. In the face of death, Richard, like any other man, becomes a child once more. We understand him and forgive him. Nobody gathers around the coffin, placed on the empty field. We hear the desert wind, while Mahalia Jackson sings a Negro spiritual called "Mother and Child."

2   Portia versus a computer.
The Merchant of Venice

Here we find something unique in all of Shakespeare. His favourite character in the play is a woman. Crowned with the glory of beauty, delicacy, and dazzling intelligence, Portia embodies what we might call the archetypal good fairy of Nordic fairy tale. A world inveterately wicked, in thrall to money, a world personified by Shylock, is transformed thanks to the intervention of a miraculous being. There are three protagonists: Antonio, the potential victim; Shylock, symbolising enslavement to gold; and Portia, the woman called upon to tame the evil spirit that has battened on another man's life.

Let us recall all the phases of the play's plot: the loan and the contract that makes Shylock demand a pound of Antonio's flesh; Portia's happy marriage and her presence, in disguise, at the trial, where she saves Antonio. Not many things happen in this Shakespearean text, but its humanism presents to us the tenderness of a woman's heart in the best possible light. The play has a majestic simplicity. Its conclusion would seem to be that in the midst of harsh laws, men will never be able to resemble a woman who opens up the path to life. Above all else, we marvel at an intervention aimed at clarifying human nature. Portia will do justice. And what justice! One and all, we will fall in love with her nature and meditate in silence for years and centuries on what the world might look like if the law was embodied by a woman. Reading Shakespeare's play, we will feel a thrill of love, born of our encounter with the main female protagonist.

I do not see any Jewish problem in this text. Shylock might equally have belonged to any other community, but his evil would still have been unshakable. Shylock's evil seems motiveless. It is primordial, it comes from the depths. It is like an envenomed blade.

How are we to represent such inhumanity theatrically? Shylock's evil is so distant from the good and the beautiful. Might it be appropriate for us to represent him as a hideous imp? No. In my opinion, the way in which he makes use of contract law to exact a pound of Antonio's flesh, the inflexibility, the coldness, the precision that characterise him in this pursuit, sooner liken him to an electronic rather than a human brain. In my production, I would have Antonio and Portia join together in a dangerous game against a highly complex computer. The precision of the computer's calculations harries Antonio, trying to destroy him. Obviously, in our century, such a problem should no longer surprise us. But of course, we will find human satisfaction when the computer that inflexibly follows a law is short-circuited, in the moment when the sentence is overturned, also by mathematical precision, this being Portia's astonishing achievement.

I don't know what will happen to Shylock after the trial, but I would like to see him as a robot whose batteries have burnt out. In this way, we will learn that in every human act and human law, there has to be a dose of tolerance, there has to come a moment when we wake up to the fact that behind the words there beats a heart that laughs and cries. Portia's beauty and wisdom are without precedent. And it is not at all a bad thing that we come to understand what a priceless treasure shines within that astonishing Eternal Feminine.

In the *Merchant of Venice*, Shakespeare goes deep into a strange theme. It seems to me that here the human is discussed via two particular concepts. We have before us the strange and fanatical face of a strict interpreter of the letter of the law and, in complete contrast, a heart and mind coloured by delicacy and goodness in the high value in which they hold the human. Now let me say why this is so. Our century has been invaded by mathematical formulas and computers. Unimaginable precision has transformed every phenomenon into a rigid structure. But what can be more at odds with this technical onslaught than a woman's understanding heart and gaze? I would like to create a production in which contradictory emotions, ease of movement, and tolerant thought come up against the hardness of iron.

For a long time, I have thought of making Shylock a computer. How satisfying we will find it when, caught in the trap of his own unforgiving logic, he short-circuits, blows a fuse! How significant Antonio's opening soliloquy will be then!

> In sooth, I know not why I am so sad:
> It wearies me; you say it wearies you;
> But how I caught it, found it, or came by it,
> What stuff 'tis made of, whereof it is born,
> I am to learn;
> And such a want-wit sadness makes of me
> That I have much ado to know myself.

Shakespeare teaches us not to forget that a man's life is not just his everyday actions, but that a large part of his life remains in the shadow. The human soul is shot through with presentments, intuitions, misunderstood fears. And often logic grips like a vice, it constrains a body and a bundle of emotions too choice and too complex to fit any pattern, even should the formula be derived from Pythagoras himself. The flow of life bursts every dam, demolishes wall after wall, wins the freedom of flight.

I would like to construct a ceremony, but one made up of contrasts between rigid gestures and emotional outbursts. The theatrical act will enable minute reflection. We will spotlight the female space of the stage, where flowers and delightful trees grow, and which is brutally separated by rusty sheet metal from the unsightly area where the gold traders keep their stalls. The music to accompany this inimical court case between human fragility and the mathematically exacting fanaticism of computerised intolerance will be endless Bach concertos. But when the final computer short-circuits, the cast will throw pine branches over the machines that have seduced civilisation and, dazzlingly garbed, they will come to the front of the stage and gaze into the eyes of the audience.

For, the human gaze can never be replaced, whether the times be inimical or whether they be beautiful. Yet again, we will be reminded of Ulysses's long journey back to Penelope, of Dante's journey to Beatrice, and we will understand what Goethe related to us about the Eternal Feminine throughout his work.

3   Under the sign of Miranda, or Swansong. *The Tempest*

The great aestheticians and art critics have wonderful things to say about Shakespeare's final play, *The Tempest*. This final dramatic text is the so-called poetic testament of the great William Shakespeare. Like any other adieu, the playwright's final message, his act of bidding the world farewell, is charged with the greatest sadness, accompanying as it does a pair of fragile wings on their final flight above the temple named the Globe Theatre. It was there, through his enthralling plays, that Shakespeare grappled with the questions of his day. The words of Prospero, in the farewell play that is *The Tempest*, are the words of an aged, weary writer, now disarmed in the midst of the people who have applauded him for a while but will soon forget him:

> I'll bring you to your ship, and so to Naples,
> Where I have hope to see the nuptial
> Of these our dear-beloved solemnised;
> And thence retire me to my Milan, where
> Every third thought shall be my grave.

The performance has ended. The old clown makes one last lap of the circus, bowing to the potentates, and then retires to his dressing room, where he takes off his face paint. From beneath the make-up, the deep wrinkles of helpless old age will reveal themselves in the mirror. As a play, *The Tempest* seems devoid of energy. It is as if the optimism that colours its words demands to be spoken in a whisper. For many years I have been thinking about the enigma contained in the text. I seek to capture it, to make it visible. On the strangeness of the play's events, one of the characters comments thus:

> Th'affliction of my mind amends, with which,
> I fear, a madness held me: this must crave—
> An if this be at all—a most strange story.

My imagination, uncovering the hidden mainsprings of Shakespeare's text, focuses on an image that I regard as a kind of archetype. It is that festive performance in which a great artist bids his peers and his faithful audience farewell. At the same time, I think of a one-act play of great refinement by Chekhov, titled *Swansong*.

A farewell performance possesses a genuine and boundless sense of tragedy. The artist is preparing to die. Jung said that old age in itself is a primordial image, in other words, an archetype. I see Prospero's final performance clearly. I imagine the great Prospero as a tragic clown whose business is taming the forces of nature. His magic endows the plants with sentiments and tames even the most savage beasts. As Nietzsche says in a book about tragedy and man, the tiger and the panther meekly lie down at the feet of man the creator. In fact, Prospero embodies the mysterious Orpheus. Entering the circus big top, I see Prospero saluting the great lords with a humble bow. The powerful watch him. They have long paid this artist to entertain them. To me, *The Tempest* becomes the ceremony that prepares the way for the playwright's passage to the next world. The magic staff will perform its last miracle: saving the helpless child from human villainy. That child is the wonderful Miranda. The old Prospero, much like the beleaguered King Lear, discovers a final reason for his art, dedicating his final wonder to his beloved daughter. Prospero addresses the powerful, requesting their protection.

In the midst of the tamed beasts, childhood and innocence will be a social shield. The world is stalked by vice, lust, lies, and deceit. What Hamlet says of Denmark remains valid to the very end of the great playwright's work.

But Miranda, unfamiliar with life, will exclaim, on seeing other humans:

> O, wonder!
> How many goodly creatures are there here!
> How beauteous mankind is! O brave new world,
> That has such people in't!

But the men Miranda sees are, as Jan Kott remarks, in fact villains. Who will protect Miranda? Who will save the child? The old clown Prospero performs the wonder with the last of his powers. But will the result be lasting? You are gripped with genuine fear. Seldom did the great Shakespeare suffer so cruelly beneath the semblance of a comedy. The suffering that grips the play is visceral. I imagine the audience of the time as being composed of lords. Like Rigoletto, Verdi's protagonist, Prospero will try to smooth brows furrowed by the lust for power. The artist bids the whole world a dignified farewell. Ultimately, it is not the beasts of the forest that will have to be tamed, but the heart of man.

I remember Chaplin's film *The Kid*, in which Charlot gives his last crust of bread to a five-year-old boy. What savage world will Miranda adopt, who has no expectations? Prospero remains powerless:

> Now my charms are all o'erthrown,
> And what strength I have's mine own,
> Which is most faint.

Alone in his hut, once the lights of enchantment are extinguished, Prospero will weep. All the tears of the world have welled beneath his eyelids. The play is over. The artist remains alone with his misery. Michelangelo has bitter words to say about the solitude of the artist who has abandoned the world. On the road of no return, he takes with him the void. But Shakespeare loved clowns. He loved those who tell the truth. Prospero is such a clown. Alongside his good heart lives the purest child of all time: Miranda. Miranda's wonderment at the beauty of mankind burns in our hearts with the blaze of red-hot iron. It travels down the ages. What might we say about her childlike exclamation if we were to juxtapose it with the sceptical thought of a Montaigne?

Prospero's solitude haunts me. Who will protect him? Prospero loved plants and animals. Miranda accompanied him in his suffering. But who will keep watch over the bitter fate of a solitary artist? Enveloped in melancholy, Prospero will bid his audience farewell. The essential question that Shakespeare asks remains unanswered. In the midst of a compassionless world, Prospero and Miranda expect compassion. A burning tear scalds the cheek. Thus, without deciding one way or the other, the author allows us to understand for ourselves that we must unreservedly embrace High Art.

4 The utopia of discontent.
As You Like It

The world is in disarray. Injustice reigns over the almost abandoned city. The people have retreated to the forest. Only a few sycophantic courtiers remain behind with the usurping duke. The two social levels are the very antithesis of each other. The world of the court and the world of freedom. This is where I might have something to say. Shakespeare doesn't darken our imagination. Horrors are absent. We find ourselves in the zodiac of Comedy. Injustice does not take a horrific guise. We hear of preparations for murder, but Orlando, the protagonist, escapes to the forest in time.

Ultimately, the world of the city is boring more than it is evil. Its entertainments and flights of imagination can be reduced to wrestling. Disinterest or the downright insipid dresses up as an old witch and roams the halls of almost deserted castles. I imagine the performance at the court as taking place in a mediaeval castle. Invited to a journey, the audience will climb out of buses and accompanied by the stage director of the performance, they will walk around a real castle. They will understand that those lifeless rooms are haunted by cold. For anybody at all, cold is a terrible punishment. In one corner, a pale woman keeps combing her dishevelled hair. A small child is being bathed in a brass vessel. But the child's mother is weeping. Terror hides its face under a veil of boredom. Nobody vociferates. They speak in whispers. What the melancholy Jacques will later say is relevant here: "It is a melancholy of mine own, compounded of many simples . . ." The two female leads, Celia and Rosalind, along with Touchstone, the beloved fool, are preparing to depart. In these parts, there is no singing, there is no theatre; it is a world that presages a harsh trial. Shakespeare suggests a cataleptic social state. Against its will, a society is forced to take part in a depressing, hideous journey of boredom. Here, absence reigns. The void looms. Mortified by disinterest, the people follow the duke on his imageless journey. Time passes like an endless ache.

Touchstone utters a censored thought: "The more pity, that fools may not speak wisely what wise men do foolishly." Then they depart. In fact, life at the castle will be an interlude for the audience; the real performance will take place in the forest. Leaving the castle, the audience will travel with the actors into the forest. We will all come to a stop in a clearing. Beneath Nature's wing, we will rejoice in the mirth of lovers who are free.

Henceforth I think of the mysterious philosophy contained in Plato's *Symposium*. A symposium takes place here in the forest. A celebration of thought. In this privileged space will be acted out an apologia for the restless and immortal Eros. I have a clear feeling of the sway that Eros holds over the folk of the Forest of Arden. They are caught up in the game. The games seem merry and innocent, but deep inside Eros there lurks a flame that consumes the life of him or her who is unaware.

There is celebration in the clearing. A company of wassailers sings of the cuckolded man. No care overshadows the playfulness. The protagonists dine on choice viands. You merely stretch out your hand to take them. Exactly the same as in the story Don Quixote tells the shepherds about the "Golden Age." Whenever anybody is hungry, he can eat his fill. We have here a great celebration of those in love. Everything takes place on a beautiful day in May, when, going into the forest, man finds relaxation listening to beautiful words of love.

Here I would have something to say. The man has long since left the city, but he senses that mediocrity has followed him like a faithful animal. This time the forms are truly animated. The party is noisy. But the time comes when terrible noonday arrives. The moment comes when the strong heat of the sun makes him sweat. Parasols and sunglasses will be brought to bear, but something will not be quite right. A doubt has insinuated itself into our game. The melancholy of Jacques is stronger than he is, and he will bring it with him to the game. A subterranean melancholy, an unconfessed sadness envelops the whole dramatic text. Once again, we hear Jacques's words: "It is a melancholy of mine own, compounded of many simples, extracted from many objects."

Through the performance I would venture to suggest that the meaning of events is somewhere deficient. The creator has set his characters in motion, they continue to perform their actions, but the creator is no longer there. The most striking sign of the void is always the mechanical toy. Shakespeare does indeed smile at the game, but I think his smile is tinged with bitterness.

The castle interlude suggested to us terror; in the forest, we are wholly free, but something is not right. Shakespeare suggests to us a doubt, a certain scepticism. The evil will become good. The usurping duke will become a monk and give away his wealth and power. The good will return to society. A question mark floats above the future. In the end, an unknown goddess urges people to take the path of love, a spiritual love that will become concrete, carnal.

But the company will still not have any specific goal. *As You Like It* seems to me a play without a solution. A strange anxiety accompanies these events and the liveliest laughter is menaced by the times that will not be long in coming. The exuberant forest seems menaced by a fast-encroaching desert. The utopia of the Forest of Arden is a performance. And every performance comes to an end. This utopia is rather sad. By understanding Jacques the melancholic, we will foresee Hamlet the malcontent.

5   *The Two Gentlemen of Verona*

If Shakespeare had written a play full of merriment, without a trace of bitterness, it would have meant the visionary discovery of a new Paradise. But it is only in utopias that the world is healed and, unfortunately, Shakespeare nowhere glimpsed any paradise without a trace of evil. *The Two Gentlemen of Verona* is a bitter comedy. In vain might we wish to discover in it a complete, exuberant, radiant joy at life. Peace and the final reconciliation arrive somewhat unexpectedly. The pure world of youth is infiltrated by something unnatural, which dangerously irradiates hearts athirst for love. Insidiously, a crisis as bitter as disease is at man's root, undermining, now the same as in the past, the aspiration to soaring flight and human perfection.

At first sight, it might seem that Shakespeare amused himself by writing a farce about the friendship between two young gentlemen. What could be worthier or more beautiful than the brotherhood of two men? And what could be merrier than when one of them cunningly fools the other? But even so, the great playwright does not stop there, now the same as in the past. The overlooked scheme occasions a bitter meditation on character whose dazzling highlights trouble us like a storm at sea. Evil seeps into the innermost places and poisons the soul's most beautiful mood, splits asunder all hope. Actions accumulate, events accelerate until a serene happy end arrives. But the reconciled smile of the wise man of Avon hides a profound shudder, accompanied by a strange disquiet, a secret fear.

If I wish to decipher the enigma of this text whose wit agitatedly beats its wings, I do so because I feel the need to talk about a certain kind of youth. The story that rustles in its depths demands an accompaniment of flames, glowing coals, love. The tremendous joke strikes me as something of genius thanks to a kind of ruthlessness that brands the most dreadful lack of all: soullessness. It seems so paradoxical that in a tissue of loving acts the heart might be absent. Wonderful in its power, Shakespearean irony selects a group of young people similar to those who set out into the silent Forest of Arden. This time, too, fools accompany their masters on their journey into the labyrinth.

The fools, brilliant messengers of lucidity, caught up in events too simple not to appear strange, play a courageous role this time, too. They comment on the actions and guises of their masters. I might say that thanks to the role they have taken on, they become so unsparing that in their coldness they resemble large mirrors following around those in desperate search of their reflections. In fact, the fool bearing a mirror has been an authentic theatrical archetype ever since the beginnings of theatre. This is how Speed answers Valentine:

Valentine: Why, how know you that I am in love?
Speed: Marry, by these special marks: First, you have learned, like Sir Protheus, to wreath your arms like a malcontent; to relish a love-song, like a robin redbreast; to walk alone, like one that had the pestilence; to sigh, like a school-boy that had lost his A.B.C.; to weep, like a young wench that had buried her grandam; to fast, like one that takes diet; to watch, like one that fears robbing; to speak puling, like a beggar at Hallowmas. you were wont, when you laughed, to crow like a cock; when you walked, to walk like one of the lions; when you fasted, it was presently after dinner; when you looked sadly, it was for want of money: and now you are metamorphosed with a mistress, that, when I look on you, I can hardly think you my master.

This dreadful image is a grotesque symbol of the face of love. It heralds themes different than those of the love between Romeo and Juliet. Dizzying contrasts mist the white lights of fever and delirium. Love is nothing but vast exhaustion. It distorts young eyes and faces. Unforgiving, the wise playwright plays with a number of deceptive appearances, transforming merry events into a tightrope-walking nightmare, something melancholy and heart-rending. A humanist, a servant of the castle, a traditional Renaissance man, will plead in vain that the young people gathered to kill time should pursue Knowledge instead:

Panthino: He wondered that your lordship
Would suffer him to spend his youth at home;
While other men, of slender reputation,
Put forth their sons to seek preferment out:
Some to the wars, to try their fortune there;
Some to discover islands far away;
Some to the studious universities.

But youth dedicates itself to love that goes hand in hand with boredom and fatality. Woman is a powerful mirage, alluring, playful, for whose sake it is worth selling your soul and your friend. A bitter lesson! The superficial women in this play are so simple that their fascination remains solely erotic. When admired, they content themselves with pleasing others, flirting, casting sly glances.

I would like to stage a performance that is like rotting lace. A performance that will make the gaze shudder. A performance that will have to have a musical accompaniment. But it will be a tenebrous, underground music. The play will be set in a meadow full of flowers, where the young lovers, smartly dressed, in the late-twentieth-century style, come to listen to music and litter the sacred space of nature with discarded beer bottles, coffee jars, and cigarettes. Dressed in jeans, afire with love, a love primarily carnal, exhausted by the void in their souls, they will throw a dark party. I think of young people, the so-called *blousons-noirs*, who one night in Paris rolled huge concrete pipes down the street for want of a better occupation. Envy, malice, lies will affectively dominate the spiritual wasteland. And at the end, putting on smoking jackets and mini bridal gowns, they will celebrate a banal wedding, in an undefined space, a time as insipid as plastic flowers. Evil deeds seem to have been driven out, but the young bride and groom, once the wedding has been celebrated, are instantly bored, with shouts of triumph, everybody jumps into a convertible car, incorrigibly devoted to nothing but pleasure.

This Shakespearean fable has a secret moral, a seductive, sad moral. I would like to put on a cruel performance, with rich kids who waste their time learning the secrets of the Eros sooner than needed. Young people full of fear and boredom. Devoid of life's youthful ferment. Seeking oblivion in depravity. Eager to shine inwardly more than for the other. Ready to sell their friends and share their lovers. This dark world will reveal within its depths a horrifying meaning that rests under the sign of the memorable line by Eminescu: "Never did I think I would learn to die . . ."

6 The comedy of history.
Julius Caesar

The deeds and actions of heroes, the words unspoken, the silence lurking in the depths, the sound and fury of war, the battle songs, the dazzling light and the menacing dark all come together in a monumental dramatic structure whose meanings Shakespeare scribbled in such a way that the audience might enter into contact with a historical process stripped down to the dimensions of a performance, experiencing its heights with a terror that won't be wearying. I am fully convinced that this play, which, in poetry and prose, debates complex confrontations, gives us occasion for a dark ceremony, but whose core is profoundly ironic. To make myself clear, I will select a few essential moments on which such a directorial concept might rest.

With diabolical skill, Shakespeare finds room within the terrifying cycle of historical events for calm, everyday moments, which make us laugh, wavering between the tragic and the ironic. No matter how grand the characters might be, no matter how much these thundering heroes might wish to impress us, with a gentle, secret smile Shakespeare gives us the opportunity to be witness to the human, all-too-human alloy of everyday and historical life.

There are two particularly beautiful moments before the assassination of Caesar. Two women appear in this tragedy of men to express their anxiety. One is Calpurnia, Caesar's wife, the other Portia, Brutus's wife. Their appearance is not gratuitous. Shakespeare knows better than anybody else that when a woman is anxious, her deep intuition senses danger by means of preternatural antennae. The two women divine the catastrophe. Compared with them, playing their roles as men of history, both Caesar and Brutus are, humanly speaking, mere children. The way in which both Caesar and Brutus dismiss their wives' advice saddens us, all the more so given that Calpurnia and Portia are women who love ardently.

Such moments, when the heroes get ready in the wings before mounting the stage of history, humanise the deficiencies of political conflict. After the death of Caesar, the inflamed Brutus makes an irreparable mistake by allowing Mark Anthony to speak to the crowd. It is decisive. Like a good father,

Shakespeare allows us to discover in Brutus a naïve man who resembles a child almost all too much, and nothing more than that. The way in which Brutus allows Mark Anthony to give a political speech to the crowd at Caesar's funeral demonstrates a candour blind to the shameless cunning of history. Mark Anthony will prove to be not only a vain ham actor, but also a skilled politician. His speech, which we summon up once more within our satirical vision, is almost grotesque, laced, I might say, with black humour.

The detailed analysis of all the wounds incurred by the now lifeless body is carried out with the meticulousness of a bureaucratic inspector at the gate of Hell. Listening to Mark Anthony, we smile in terror: "Look! in this place, ran Cassius' dagger through: / See, what a rent the envious Casca made; / Through this the well-beloved Brutus stabbed, / And as he plucked his cursed steel away, / Mark how the blood of Caesar followed it." The details of this disturbing autopsy will rouse the fury of the mob. Mark Anthony has found a cunning way of reversing their attitude toward the conspirators. The mob runs riot through Rome. Shakespeare sends a small, fearful man into their path:

Third Citizen:	Your name, Sir, truly.
Cinna:	Truly, my name is Cinna.
First Citizen:	Tear him to pieces: he's a conspirator.
Cinna:	I am Cinna the poet; I am Cinna the poet.
Fourth Citizen:	Tear him for his bad verses; tear him for his bad verses.

We are moved by the fate of the poor, talentless poet. But we smile with solemn sadness: in the face of brute force, all poetry is worthless. Words become powerless and helpless man perishes like a gnat. Shakespeare, the great master of choice ceremonies, ironically commenting on history, guides us down the path of farce.

As a director I feel the need to bring on stage large brass bands to accompany this performance that oscillates between horror and smiles. The conspiracy will fail. But before the great battle, before the clash of armies, before the war, Brutus, getting ready for bed in his tent, will utter a line essential to our vision of the play: "Lucius, my gown." We can hardly believe it. The hero asks for his nightgown. In no other tragedy does Shakespeare treat his heroes with such trenchant irony:

Brutus:	Everything is well.
Cassius:	Good night, my lord.
Brutus:	Good night, good brother.
Titinius and Messalia:	Good night, lord Brutus.
Brutus:	Farewell, every one.

This bedtime litany will surely make us smile. This terrible tragedy contains within its dark substance magical stereotypes. Through repetition, the final suicides, like a string of beads, one after the other, no matter how grand they are intended to be, become not only strange, but also comical, but it is black comedy, which only reinforces the boundaries of the tragic. Brought to light, the secret mechanism of history causes the pomp and glory of the heroes to fall away; now they are but fragile men, with all their tics.

I would like my performance to unfold within a Roman circus. The same place where gladiators savagely sacrifice themselves, slaughtering each other for the sadistic pleasure and joy of the emperors. The viewpoint, the directorial attitude, will be that of goading the irrational impulses of history. In the arena, exaggeratedly made-up clowns will rush in, thrilling us like the actors at the end of Antonioni's *Blow Up*, driven along the empty streets of a provincial town in a minibus. At the end of our performance, a woman dressed in black clothes, like a Salvation Army uniform, will step over the corpses. She will passionately sing a song made up of the final lines about Brutus.

7   *Much Ado About Nothing*

At the beginning, a messenger informs us of a war that has just come to an end. The protagonists about to enter the stage one by one earned military glory in the final battle. The women slyly inquire about them, displaying a kind of boredom, a dissimulated distraction. The knights return from the war. An irrational war, like all wars. Those who enter the stage, to cheers and applause, are men who have killed.

Once the war is over, the fighters will spend their lives in peace and quiet. Is Shakespeare simplifying life? Not at all. For life without war can unfold in only one way. Here, on the threshold between war and peace, appears Woman, in decadent splendour, offering herself to the warrior returning from battle. A woman whose eyes gleam, like Beatrice's, or a woman who murmurs naïve prayers, like Hero. The text is suggestive to me of a strange ritual. What secret does the story conceal, what hidden meaning lurks therein?

The warriors, knights of war, devoid of elegant manners, roughhewn men, alleviate their boredom by fathering children, by loving, by marrying. The scenario really does seem completely ordinary, I might even say, banal. But a dangerous, unforgiving demon cunningly insinuates itself into the torpor of everyday events. Something vague, ambiguous, something that has the sterile whiff of futility, accompanies the ceremony of time, preventing any reinvigoration, allowing only the eternal somnolence of the stereotypical, as if a magical, fascinating banality marked time for the choice couples. Everything takes place at a strictly everyday level. Somebody even says what date it is: 6 July. Out of boredom, a malevolent person hatches an infamy. As a result, the bride will be rejected at the altar on moral grounds. A minor provincial drama. But the calumny is exposed and everything ends happily, in over-the-top joyousness. The wedding finally takes place. The intriguer is apprehended. This final piece of news might have been overlooked, but it is precisely here that the demon makes its appearance, a mental state that augurs ill. But here are the final lines: "*Messenger*: My lord, your brother John is ta'en in flight, / And brought with armed men back to Messina. *Benedick*: Think not on him till tomorrow: I'll devise thee brave punishments for him. Strike up, pipers. [*Dance. Exeunt*]"

Benedick is a soldier by profession. We know this. But when such a Shakespearean character promises "brave punishments," we shudder. From somnolence, from beneath banal appearances, something momentarily awakes and keeps us waiting with baited breath. The life unfolding before us is not so innocent as it might have seemed at first sight. The stage remains empty at the end. In no case should the lights come on to announce the end of the performance. It must be implied that the sacred, metaphysical space of the stage will "tomorrow" become the torture chamber where Benedick and other soldiers will amuse themselves with their captive. You blink, as if having awoken at midnight.

It is from this directorial motif that I would proceed in imagining my production of this play. I see the events as if they were crammed into the interval of a respite. Between two battles, between two wars, it is not a bad thing to start a family. A cruel irony. You will perhaps be more courageous on the battlefield knowing that someone will mourn you should you die. I imagine a stage dotted with soldiers. Clumsy warriors, full of candour, comical in their seriousness, they will act like diligent pupils, without any great enthusiasm, performing everything necessary.

But the initial return from the war should not be forgotten for a single moment. I would like to present and develop these hints of war and military order, to have them surround the sacred wedding that is being planned. As a result, the unnatural infiltrates all the gestures of the everyday. The characters cease to experience actions emotionally. The ceremony will be like the action of a mechanical toy. A mechanical game that is experienced as such within a fascinated awareness. A terrible anguish sweeps the space, harrowing the people, who in their desperation attempt to forget everything, casting themselves into the masked ball of the second act. There will be no miracle, and the people, regarding their entertainment as mediocre, will content themselves with scandal accompanied by boredom and mediocre merriment. Let there be a ball! Even if the soldiers will wound the heart of the bride at the altar, a bride who is obviously grotesque.

A stray friar's plea for innocence makes our hearts shudder and laugh thanks to words that transcribe a real moment of dull purity, that of a Madonna swathed in mist, vanishing as if it were not fitting that we should mention it in a world all too insensible, itself a symbol of living at the physiological level:

> Hear me a little;
> For I have only been silent so long,
> And given way unto this course of fortune,
> By noting of the lady: I have marked
> A thousand blushing apparitions
> To start into her face; a thousand innocent shames
> In angel whiteness beat away those blushes;
> And in her eye there hath appeared a fire,
> To burn the errors that these princes hold
> Against her maiden truth.

These lines and this speech I see accompanied by mad merriment. Delirious, aggressive humour is needed in order to depict such a world full of soldiers and too innocent brides. A merry, waggish world, prone to fooling people and to being fooled. I am thinking here of the commentative attitude toward characters who are submerged in the sensory and emptied of thought, as Breughel depicts them in his paintings. At the same time, I think of a performance close to the naïve paintings of the Balkan peoples.

What conclusion might be drawn from such a performance? I don't think that such a vision, a vision of a world that is bored of living and sees life as banal, could be very far from today's psychological needs. On the contrary. By rebound, the life protected by Peace would rediscover its energy and inherent joys. I think of a performance of Brecht's *Mutter Courage* that I saw via a film by the Berliner Ensemble. Even today, I still remember the suggestions the performance gave me.

And so, I see the end of my production of *Much Ado About Nothing* as follows: After the characters leave the stage according to Shakespeare's direction, after a pause of a minute, from the distance can be heard, softly at first, then louder and louder, a beating drum, then a bugle, after which the soldiers and their officers grimly rush back onstage for a new war, forced to run and to fall in line, abandoning lovers, wives, children, forced to leave their gardens, beds, feasts, even their privies, a grotesque, torturous sight, at this dangerous, irritating, terrifying bugle call of all the centuries in history, which have never quelled the wars that always knock on the doors of the world with the rapping of Satan, accompanied by laughter and fear.

8   The man without qualities, or, *The Comedy of Errors*

This is an ambiguous comedy. Like a hunter trailed by his footprints in the snow, the situations that are positively comical will be trailed by a drama that is sinister. A drama that will unfold in secret chambers. The merchants of Syracuse caught in Ephesus will be taken away to be executed. Against this dark, death-bringing background, I therefore wonder what meaning the mix-up between the master twins and the servant twins might have? In imagining my performance, I am tempted to set out from the strange line spoken by one of the characters: "There's something in the wind / That we cannot get in." What is in the wind? What is it that he senses in the air? Danger, evidently. The same character will later recount:

> then, all together,
> They fell upon me, bound me, bore me thence,
> And in a dark and dankish vault at home
> There left me . . .

Such irruptions of violence are terrifying. The violence that marked Shakespeare's times is typical of the twentieth century too. What then does the character sense on the wind? A threat. But from whom? It is by setting out from this lurking menace, which can be sensed only in a parapsychological moment, that I wish to define the meaning of my performance. I think that light is the most sensible element of danger. There is a fluctuating relationship between danger and light. Light is transformed in relation to any danger. This is why I picture a huge searchlight above this small ghost town. A bright flash, a magical flicker, marks hours of the day. In the heart of the town pulses an electronic clock. Gripped with fear, Adriana will say, in amazement: "The hours come back!"

In regard to the luminous signal, let me quote what is to me a key line for the performance I imagine. Toward the end, an abbess speaks from the wise viewpoint of those who oversee equilibrium:

> In food, in sport, and life-preserving rest,
> To be disturbed would mad or man or beast.

This hint of some harmful psychological experiment is alarming. Somewhere, the intuited danger is skilfully concealed and we will witness a violent, complex progression, which is not just comical, but tragic. In this comedy there appears a deep, disquieting archetype. A man is revealed minute by minute, accompanied by *his double*. Whoever has looked in the mirror for a long time and been frightened at the thought that someone with the same face is looking back at him from the depths will understand this subtle and insinuating suggestion with which Shakespeare shatters the peace and tranquillity of the comedy. The author smiles a secret smile behind the symbolic situation. I think that for any one of us the thought of having an identical double not only makes us laugh, but terrifies us. Edgar Allan Poe minutely examines the strangeness of such a situation.

In my performance, the idea of the "man without qualities" will be the central theme, an idea central to the work of both Musil and Kafka. What occurs will be almost demonic. I would like to suggest that such events take place in a technologically advanced society. Everywhere will be seen radars and strange mechanisms to control people's voices and images. For a stranger arriving in Ephesus, the city will seem sinister. Antipholus of Syracuse describes it thus:

> They say this town is full of cozenage;
> As nimble jugglers, that deceive the eye,
> Dark-working sorcerers, that change the mind,
> Soul-killing witches, that deform the body,
> Disguised cheaters, prating mountebanks,
> And many such like liberties of sin.

To me, Shakespeare's stage direction that the Duke is attended by the Headsman and other Officers is of the essence. We find ourselves in a dictatorial society. The bloody law of the city weighs on ordinary events, imbuing them with wretchedness. I think of the way in which the characters will move around the stage. The overall impression is one of structural anxiety. The small town with its coloured radars will look grey. The people's costumes will be too nondescript to attract attention. A crowd of grey, mediocre people, deprived of entertainments, forced to stay inside the city, are subjected to a baneful political fate, and it is in this context that the case of mistaken identity involving Antipholus will occur. It is time to ask ourselves whether certain social conventions of the citizens of Ephesus are natural.

I imagine a performance in a manner reminiscent of the style of Alain Robbe-Grillet's novels. The walls of the barracks along which walks the soldier in his novel *The Labyrinth* will provide an essential image for my performance. The audience will adopt a subjective viewpoint, the same as in the art of the film. We will view events from the psychological angle of the victim. For, there is a victim. At the end, Antipholus of Ephesus will lament the sorry events of his life. As elsewhere, Shakespeare's smile is bitter. But from the darkness of bitterness a fresh tendril sprouts. A stellar light pierces the darkness: Adriana's love. Let us listen to her monologue, with the thought that nowhere is woman more beautiful than in this metaphor that has come down to us across the centuries:

> Come, I will fasten on this sleeve of thine;
> Thou are an elm, my husband; I, a vine,
> Whose weakness, married to thy stronger state,
> Makes me with thy strength to communicate.

And perhaps the question addressed to the wife of Antipholus of Syracuse will become a certainty in our performance: "Are you a god?"

If the world created by men is corrupt and unjust, in the heart of woman there flickers a secret hope. Years and centuries of love are in preparation. And is not a solution suggested to us enclosed within a prayer? The male/female antithesis will be transformed into a primordial relationship. In speaking to the woman, Antipholus relinquishes his world:

> Teach me, dear creature! how to think and speak;
>   Lay open to my earthy gross conceit,
> Smothered in errors, feeble, shallow, weak,
>   The folded meaning of your words' deceit.

Among soldiers, immaculately garbed, the woman will bring with her the light of a starry sky.

9 *Love's Labour's Lost*

A comedy brushed by the heavy wing of bitterness. Perhaps in no other Shakespearean text is more enigmatic a contrast at work. What I mean is that in this disturbing comedy there occurs a strange, powerful clash between man and woman. A band of young nobles led by the King of Navarre makes almost a sacred covenant. They decide to embark on three years of stark asceticism. The young men dedicate themselves to books heart and soul. Their lofty covenant elevates strict, assiduous book learning to an almost divine level. It seems that no obstacle can stand in the way of their decision:

> Therefore, brave conquerors, for so you are,
> That war against your own affections,
> And the huge army of the world's desires,
> Our late edict shall strongly stand in force;
> Navarre shall be the wonder of the world;
> Our court shall be a little Academe,
> Still and contemplative in living art.

Nonetheless, this strict canon will be violently shaken. Who will conquer study, books, or meditation on the world's meanings? The young men will admit defeat, bemoaning their fate in desperate, almost embarrassing confessions. They have not yet even begun to search for the abstruse laws of art and science. They have merely taken the decision to dedicate themselves to learning. The untamed enemy of language and meaning proves to be Woman. It is interesting that among Shakespeare's noble characters can be found pseudo-scholars of language and learning, whose function is to caricature the fanatical impulse toward art and science.

Supposed cultural initiates such as Don Adriano de Armado, Sir Nathaniel, and Holofernes express themselves so pretentiously that we can see through the fog the future that is in store for the young noblemen who abnegate life for the sake of learning. Once woman is introduced into this complex comedy, the result is fascinating.

The princess who is heir to the throne of France and her three ladies in waiting will confound the minds of the young noblemen. The hidden meaning, the enigma of Shakespeare's text, obsesses me. As always, Shakespeare displays ruthlessness. The defeat of the male will be an agony of nature. Destiny will make the young nobles, along with the King of Navarre, sorely atone for their having taken the wrong path.

The comedy grows darker, displaying inner ferment that sometimes causes outright pain. I would like to explain a feeling that becomes dominant in my reading of the text. I might say that the young scholars' throes of love are depicted with embarrassment. Then there is the strange way in which Shakespeare presents the women who have conquered the solitude of the scholars of Navarre.

I am not mistaken in emphasising their malicious verve, their lack of sympathy, even their ruthlessness. In control of the situation, the women of *Love's Labour's Lost* make the men bow before them, they humiliate them, impose conditions on them, then suggest a situation that will last a long while. Conquered, almost drained of strength, the men become slaves to love. Almost uniquely in Shakespeare's comedies, the ending is darkened: news of the death of the King of France arrives and the princess and her ladies in waiting declare a year of mourning before leaving Navarre. We will never know what happens next. We have taken part in a war, a battle, an archetypal duel. We will be able to understand the play and the performance only by meditating on the division of the world into male versus female.

I would like to construct a melancholy performance, wiser than it is merry. Let the enigma be contained in each image of the initial war. I would take white clothes as a symbol of the pure learning proposed by the young company from Navarre. I would have the king and his attendants be pure, immaculate, deliberately aloof from the evils of the world, having entered labyrinths illumined by wise decisions, among the ranks of the great ascetics of art and science.

I would have the action take place among dozens of mirrors. It is here that the young ladies will make their entrance, dressed showily, gaudily, with abundant lace, bracelets, petticoats, pearls, fans, extravagant hats. The mirrors will reflect the faces and enchanting toilettes, throwing overboard every effort toward knowledge and perfection. Book learning will be trampled underfoot. This parable arose from a joke. Its nobility resided in balance. The stinging aim of the comedy will be to depict the third human type, the ragged scholar skilled at discourse: Don Adriano de Armado, Sir Nathaniel, and Holofernes. It is in their lamentable pettiness that the moral of our story lies. Pedantic, incoherent, grotesque, far from the eternally human, from their words wells up a terrifying and yet, at the same time, comical nothingness:

Holofernes: Most barbarous intimation! yet a kind of insinuation, as it were, *in via*, in way, of explication; *facere*, as it were, replication, or, rather, *ostentare*, to show, as it were, his inclination, after his undressed, unpolished, uneducated, unpruned, untrained, or, rather, unlettered, or ratherest, unconfirmed fashion, to insert again my *haud credo* for a deer.

What is so appallingly depressing in this discourse is the measurable distance between people and language. The word in itself is dead; it requires the life of the human soul. And perhaps the war between words and woman will finally be won by the at times dark joke of the playwright who, in his genius, glimpsed the so-called modern crisis of language.

The women will leave the stage in mourning, with promises of future marriage. And with them vanishes the joy and the frenzy of the game. Since both before the arrival of Woman and after her departure, the characteristic mood of the play was and will be listlessness. In my production, I would like untold energies to burst into life during the ludic battle. The merry war has a rhythm, it is a dance, a cry, a pantomime, *élan vital*. The stage will be flooded with the pleasure of the battle, insane in its rhythm. The women will move as if to the rhythm of a dance, they will gesticulate energetically, they will live every moment of life to its fullest. As musical accompaniment, I might even use African drumming to evidence authentic joy in life. They will leave behind them an emptiness, an absence in the form of pain. It is now time to recall how the play ends. In the mirrors, the ragged scholars will be reflected as the solitary men of Navarre. And when their images coalesce, we will notice, too late, that the women have discreetly left.

Left to themselves, the young men will sigh, only now will they open their books, the way the teacher in Mihail Sebastian's *The Star Without a Name* opens his astronomy book. The hope of future love will cast its glow over their reading, and now the mirrors will move aside to reveal a silver tree: the tree of hidden knowledge, the metaphysical sign of the knowledge of good and evil in the vast human world.

10 Appearance and essence in *A Midsummer Night's Dream*

> The dusk of the world's time moves toward night.
>
> Heidegger

Perhaps never have we glimpsed Shakespearean joy so pure and full as in this exuberant affirmation of midnight. I would even go so far as to say that the playwright's brow and eyes are perhaps too serene as he supervises this delightful game, fascinating in its playfulness. The thoughts are as limpid as a mountain stream. But such limpidity is a bad sign. The bold Puck, master of comic entanglements, is the thread that runs through this complex weave of situations. He is a child of his time, although one that has grown old in the exercise of his profession. We take pleasure in the text of *A Midsummer Night's Dream*, which at first sight seems a merry history written in order to banish hideous sadness to the dark depths farthest from what it is to be human: "Come now; what masques, what dances shall we have, / To wear away this long age of three hours / Between our after-supper and bedtime?"

More insistently than ever before, Shakespeare tells us how beautiful is the purpose of theatre. The play is in fact an apologia for theatrical performance: the whole of the fifth act is given over to a play within the play. Nowhere else, except perhaps in *Hamlet*, does the cue for the players to make their entrance sound more vibrant than when Theseus commands: "Go, bring them in: and take your places, ladies."

I don't really understand those who see in the play the sum of our own age's erotic obsessions. The Eros that is here drolly debated is sweet, cloying, nacreous, as flimsy as a seraphic veil. I'm not at all afraid of the tender, crystalline grace that might accompany a play seemingly written for children. Why should we fear a double game? Shakespeare himself filters every word through the concept of play. Nowhere does he manifest himself with more febrile playfulness than here. It might seem that all the evils of the world have been banished by a magic spell. But there is a shameless

merriment that dances exhaustingly, almost senselessly, throughout. Why?
Merely to drive out dark thoughts? Perhaps. Once again, from our first reading of the play we are won over by a grand faith in the divine equilibrium of
the world. It might seem that we have no other hope than a performance that
will have to be the most pleasant of entertainments. Bloody power struggles
have faded away. The folk of *A Midsummer Night's Dream* love. Even if the
lovers suffer misfortunes, all turns out well and happiness crowns the most
beautiful ending of any of Shakespeare's plays:

Oberon: To the best bride-bed will we,
             Which by us shall blessed be;
             And the issue there create
             Ever shall be fortunate.
             So shall all the couples three
             Ever true in loving be;
             And the blots of Nature's hand
             Shall not in their issue stand.

Nothing could be simpler, at first sight, but . . . and it is by way of this "but"
that we shall gradually move from the space of innocence toward something
subtler, something understated and cunning, which slips among the folds of
the play's immaculate garb. This too-beautiful joy draws into its pure space
an evil shadow. Why? We shall see.

First of all, I let myself be deceived by a too-beautiful dream. Before all
else we ought to make an inventory of the garments of a blessed world, a
world so fortunate that it risks becoming unreal. All of a sudden, it is as
if we awake. Beneath this crust of overwhelming joy, a waggish demon
winks at us. And in an instant, we understand that wherever the human is
on the verge of gaining happiness, a nameless something arises, but which
despises this too-noble peace of the soul. Dialectically, in the unlit corners
of the world there lurk forces opposed to an equilibrium too easily won. It
is a demon that goes hand in hand with every human victory. But at first,
we will find no room for it in this Shakespearean world of play. We will
be forced to continue to bear the joy of playfulness. It is as if Shakespeare
is laughing at us. But elsewhere in the wide world, children are dying of
hunger. Becoming aware of our contemporary world, a world cruelly riven
by strife, the game will take on a different aspect. It is in this instant that I
become obsessed with the falsity of the maniacal clowns in Chaplin's *The
Circus*. Their playfulness is almost frightening, and in my head, I hear the
musical accompaniment to the too-happy world of *A Midsummer Night's
Dream*. What is required is an acute feeling of vanity. When will we be able
to occupy our minds only with the love so richly deserved by woman in her

fundamental eternity? When will we have the respite to know ourselves? Today's world and all its imminent dangers does not allow us to forget. We cannot deceive our grim age with good jokes.

This is why in its meaning I seek a world free of care, in a way I make solid the diaphanous veil that shrouds the dark essence of midnight. We will easily find a too-happy world, but which is aggrieved by sterility and purchased with heavy gold. I think of that strange scene in a novel by Hemingway: a young girl by a swimming pool is so terribly bored that she invents the game of taking a bite of chocolate and then swallowing it underwater. The world I see here suffers from the heaviness of time. Perhaps in no other play by Shakespeare does time pass so slowly. Four acts contain a single night.

I would create a performance that borrowed the laziness of this too-happy world that can find no entertainment for itself. A world so artificial that it makes you shudder; a world in which, out of boredom, young girls dye their hair red or green. I picture costumes painted like phosphorescent moths of ill omen. The night of a psychedelic carnival. Sterile, obsessed with physical sensation. A night in which pairs of lovers are absurdly mixed up. Merry appearances, as cunning as the devil's eye, conceal spiritual poverty and the absence of any moral order.

The characters wait for time to pass, like the two tramps waiting for Godot. We witness a celebration, an endless party. In the Middle Ages, Hell was depicted as a wassail without end. The loss of time, the sterile passage of day and night, is frightening. No fruitful outcome, no purposeful effort, no flicker of awareness comes to awaken the sleeping spirit. Idleness causes the characters to float, to give themselves up to the flow, to be dominated by anybody and anything at all, by sleep, by chasing a lover, by the games of Oberon and Puck, by the story itself, this cunning fairy tale and its occurrences, which is transformed into a parable of time, of wasted hours. Something sickly surrounds the protagonists and dwells within them. Idleness and unawareness are perilous. Empty inside, the protagonists are set in motion by chemical substances. Floral essences are administered to them. Perhaps nowhere else do we intuit so closely the robotic mechanism that is a human being. Devoid of personality, the protagonists mistake each other, they get mixed up with each other, their feelings are instantly altered, and thereby they become symbols of modern man without qualities.

Who is Oberon and who Puck in such circumstances? Perhaps we are dealing with an evil scientist, a common type in science fiction. Rather like Frankenstein, Oberon experiments on human beings, he experiments on them with chemicals, he plays with the sacrosanct human organism, altering its reactions. He dares to sully the divine substance of human blood. What happens to the human beings in *A Midsummer Night's Dream*? Once analysed critically, it is terrifying. The joke is transformed, the comedy takes on tragic overtones, it accumulates deeper meanings. The audience will be left with the impression of a Nordic fairy tale, based on the modern idea of the entropy to which human structures are prey, which in essence is an attitude of alarm at the stripping of all sacral meaning from human beings. We wish only for an inner awakening of conscious luminosity through demonstration of our unconscious failure. And perhaps thereby we will understand Oberon's final lines as the most intransigent aspersions cast against man. Oberon's world will be revealed to us as grandiose and terrifying, a world in which man is controlled and has not one jot of freedom; a world in which even procreation, the very level of the genetic, is managed.

From this viewpoint, Oberon's song becomes sombre: "To the best bridebed will we, / Which by us shall blessed be." Proceeding hence, the joke is no longer any ordinary joke. The audience will sense the allure of a diabolical mechanism. A grim gamester mistakes human beings for skittles. My production will therefore speak of an empire in which absolute terror and human idleness are woven together in a kind of performance reminiscent of both Nordic fairy tale and visionary science fiction.

11 Love and mediocrity. *Romeo and Juliet*

Every word, just like every deed, obliges us to choose among multiple alternatives, and in so choosing, we set our mode of being on a particular path. In this way, what happens to us through deeds done and words uttered becomes irreversible. We always find ourselves at a crossroads of words and deeds. If we take the wrong road, the garden of peace withers, like paper shrivelling next to a naked flame. More often than not, we regret what happens to us, as if we would wrestle with the past. But we alone must bear the brunt of the blame. By fate, everything occurs only once and this is why we bear a responsibility for words and deeds, for our thousands of words and dozens of deeds. To me, *Romeo and Juliet* is a long meditation on not paying attention. The decisions taken cannot be reversed and the words once spoken belong to the past. Dreadful irreversibility, engendered through rage and hatred, animating the present, blights the future with its fevered, agonised regret. The passions are blind and this world, which knows no rest, dancing wildly on the summits of abjection, is too vulgar to shelter a delicate creature such as love and tenderness. Around the young lovers revolves a carousel of savage satyrs in the grip of fury, whose only aim is to shed blood. A hidden, unintelligible fury, a base hatred animates the world of a small provincial town, like a hereditary curse passed down to members of a tribe now inveterate in their evil. No matter where you look, a malefic spirit winks at you, as if jokingly instigating murder. You get the feeling that people have taken leave of their senses.

At one point, Juliet's father addresses his daughter, wrathfully calling her "carrion." We give a start, as if a bucket of slops had been cast in our face. I reread the lines, unable to believe it:

> Out, you green-sickness carrion! out, you baggage!
> Your tallow-face!

Setting out from these lines, I imagine a performance in which the world is defined by vile filth. No flower blooms in this anonymous provincial town.

Moral squalor roams the streets in the guise of an old witch wearing a long cloak of black feathers. Money holds sway over men and dictates their every urge. Even instinct has been perverted. This is what Romeo tells the apothecary from whom he buys the poison:

> There is thy gold; worse poison to men's souls,
> Doing more murders in this loathsome world,
> Than these poor compounds that thou may'st not sell:
> I sell thee poison, thou hast sold me none.

We find ourselves in a world in which love is peddled for gold. This world is so petty that it is unable to tolerate so much as a crumb of real love. Glory belongs to none. Every summit is deserted. I would work with the scenographer to create the harsh image of a petty market town. The colours have faded from people's clothes. All around, there are grey houses, overrun with mould, with bars on their doors and windows, guarded by armed servants. A world of petty merchants, interested in nothing but gain, trade, pecuniary striving. The hatred between the two rival families is hereditary, traditional, exhausting. Vulgarity and insignificance have made their nest in wilted souls. The old witch, the incarnation of Satan, haunts nasty nooks and crannies. The sun rarely shows itself above this forgotten corner of the world. Tastelessness, joylessness, all the squalor of the petty have found their place on the market stalls of this dour town. What might happen here? Almost nothing. Nevertheless, a beautiful flower, threatened by the curse and the hatred, has timidly sprouted in this dank place. I see this fairy tale as Nordic rather than Mediterranean. The love of these two children, Romeo and Juliet, is accompanied by feverishness. A disquiet, a bitter presentiment, is with them from the very beginning. Around their circle of love and peace, negative forces lie in wait, ready to destroy them. This is why they hurry, as if stalked by unseen eyes.

What is to be done? Nothing. The tragedy follows its inexorable course. We all know it by heart. It has become common property. We remember in detail all its phases. The death of Mercutio. The death of Tybalt. The exile of Romeo. Juliet's forced marriage to Paris. The sleep of Juliet. The death of Romeo and then of Juliet. What meaning do these events hold for us? I think that this tragedy, more than the others, crowns a model of comportment. The beautiful love between Romeo and Juliet, as pure as a mountain stream, is exemplary. The tragedy thereby becomes a lesson. The hideousness of the parents stands as a fundamental sign. Shakespeare takes the side of the two children. He would like to protect them, so too would we, but it is not in our power. The light will go out and, in the tragedy, the fundamental mediocrity will dominate, will be triumphant. I picture the faces of the braggarts, the gluttons, the vainglorious, the vulgar, the villains, with their mediocre ways; I picture the money that rules this insignificant town. Defenceless, the two children will die. But a miracle happens. The forces of evil realise the evil they have done and the good they have lost. In this way, the model of comportment comes down through the ages.

The play will form the archetype of tragic love. As a director, I would be interested in staging the events of the play like actions filmed in slow motion, emphasising the difference between the delicate and the mediocre. The peace treaty that man has signed with impudent mediocrity terrifies me. Franco Zeffirelli created a film about the colourful world of the Renaissance. My production will take a different path. A small mediaeval German burg will be the concrete image of a world of mediocrity, made up of hundreds of functionaries. An austere, Kafkaesque bureaucracy will provide the cruel underpinning of fate. This is the world that will sign the death warrant of the two children. Romeo and Juliet remain two immortalities, two eternities to us. But how will the Prince be presented in the weave of events? He who administers justice will be a Knight of the Round Table, a kind of god in golden armour, but who cannot control a world that has gone off the rails. The Knight of Justice is almost overwhelmed by events. His words in the last scene are significant:

> A glooming peace this morning with it brings;
> The sun, for sorrow, will not show his head:
> Go hence, to have more talk of these sad things;
> Some shall be pardon'd, and some punished:
> For never was a story of more woe
> Than this of Juliet and her Romeo.

After which Shakespeare gives the stage direction: *Exeunt*. But where will they go, those who have killed love? Accompanied by a god, the Prince, they will set out on the road of endless remorse. Justice, in golden raiment, will share out gifts and punishments. But the empty stage will slowly light up, bathed in the rays of a cold sun that sheds a metaphysical light.

12   The sacrificed bride, or the symmetries of justice. *King John*

As ever, Shakespeare conceals himself behind life's events as he tells his tale. A violent, tumultuous life, rising to the heights or plunging to the depths of suffering and injustice. The tale is constructed around just a few characters: kings and their courtiers. Time's merciless juggernaut rolls over people's lives. The motivation is typical: the thirst for power. Nevertheless, Shakespeare here juxtaposes cruel events with an ineffable vagueness. But this time, there is something different about it all, and this something brings its own enigmatic flow.

Closer to the heart, the sacred seat of outraged feelings, the historical motivation is transformed into a family drama. The tragedy is engendered by the emotive alertness of events that direct, demolish, destroy a family only just setting foot on history's stage. Strange, unfathomable, destiny creates ferocious symmetries. The reader, chilled by the grim presence of lurking evil, might seek comfort in closing the book, in escaping from the play.

But in the theatre, participation in the ritual demands the reader's presence. I think that in this text evil is as dark as the shadow of night. Even so, something pure and emotive shines for an instant, it glints, flashes, vanishes. The symmetries remain sombre, grey. The main plot concerns the war for the crown and the rights of kingship. But strangely, the conflicting King John and his nephew Arthur each has his mother on his side. This war involves the one being who stands above the filth of history: the mother. The moment when Lady Constance loses her son is among the most heartrending to be found in Shakespeare. Let us listen to the wail of grief. A mother has no words to express the grief that wracks her when she loses her child, but what Lady Constance says expresses the revolt of each and every one of us. Let us listen to a mother keening for her child sacrificed by the blind instruments of history and let us think of the harrowing faces of all the mothers who wander the field after the battle is over.

Death, death, O amiable lovely death!
Thou odoriferous stench! sound rottenness!
Arise forth from the couch of lasting night,
Thou hate and terror to prosperity,
And I will kiss thy detestable bones,
And put my eyeballs in thy vaulty bones,
And ring these fingers with thy household worms,
And stop this gap of breath with fulsome dust,
And be a carrion monster like thyself.
Come, grin on me; and I will think thou smil'st,
And buss thee as thy wife! Misery's love,
O, come to me!

The tragedy is heightened through the ruthless sacrifice of a child: Arthur. Shakespeare allows the electrifying thread of confrontations to unravel. He gradually reveals the terrifying mechanism placed in the service of unjust kingship. What seems to me characteristic is that throughout the play, the historical characters speak more than is necessary. The copious and more often than not pointless words create a sense of redundancy. Not all that is communicated is essential. The characters thereby become familiar, closer to us. It is easier for us to tolerate idle chatterers. Words devoid of content create less anxiety than unfathomable silence. A silent man is terrifying. That which is hidden, concealed, bears secret weapons, capable of any deed. It is easier to tolerate a talker. But let us listen, if we dare, to the obverse of normal communication. Here, King John plans the murder of an innocent child:

Or if that thou couldst see me without eyes,
Hear me without thine ears, and make reply
Without a tongue, using conceit alone,
Without eyes, ears, and harmful sound of words:
Then, in despite of brooded, watchful day,
I would into thy bosom pour my thoughts.

We witness a terrible moment, in which the king demands that one of his henchmen understand telepathically that he wishes the child dead. It is a commonplace that murderers are silent and conceal their dark intent. The king too is unnerved by the "harmful sound of words" and "watchful day." When a man kills, the sustaining combination of word and light collapses for him. Over the course of the performance that I imagine, I would like the light gradually to fade, until by the end the play is acted by candlelight and the words are spoken with increasing weariness. Murder causes the cosmic order to collapse like a house of cards. Every value is consumed by the flames, and nature mourns her crowning glory: man. Time weeps like a child for the murdered life. In Shakespeare, words are often as terrifying as they are beautiful. Murderers understand each other by a look. I can almost picture the king accompanied by his servant, when he makes use of those cursed code words:

King John: Death.
Hubert: My lord!
King John: A grave.
Hubert: He shall not live.
King John: Enough.

In any event, Shakespeare tells us, coded language represents alienation.

Every deed, just and unjust, is bounded in the same huge shell. Destiny roars like a winter gale whose wind tears open the door of a defenceless house. People die, but still there is something, like a just and unbridled judgement, which creates strange, punitive symmetries. The unbounded swallows up, quenches every flame of rage or revolt. The old bell ringer, gravedigger Time, smiles majestically, immovable. The wind will accompany the characters through the desert, shrieking like a bird of the night. In this tragedy of helplessness, Shakespeare transcribes, with the clear eye of a night pilot, the cruel sensuousness that can be found in creatures that do evil and in the world that surrounds them. Both the atmosphere and the breath suddenly grow faint. A dangerous, unseen witness is sensed:

> Now, by my life, this day grows wondrous hot;
> Some airy devil hovers in the sky.

I would like the performance I envisage to suggest the plague knocking at the gates of a terrified and suspicious world.

> My lord, they say five moons were seen tonight:
> Four fixed, and the fifth did whirl about
> The other four in wondrous motion.

The people are seen as a superstitious mass, helpless before every form of tyranny:

> I find the people strangely fantasied,
> Possessed with rumours, full of idle dreams;
> Not knowing what they fear, but full of fear.

The wider world around the central family is barely mentioned in passing. Destiny displays its cruel arms, creeping into secret chambers and the king's tents on the battlefield. The tragedy tightly encloses the ill-starred family.

In the play there is a silent, unbearable moment when King John discovers that his mother has died. He addresses the messenger who has brought him ill tidings of the war:

> Where is my mother's care,
> That such an army could be drawn in France,
> And she not hear of it?

The reply has the tenderness of a final memory and the horror of the irremediable:

> My liege, her ear
> Is stopped with dust; the first of April died
> Your noble mother. And, as I hear, my lord,
> The Lady Constance in a frenzy died
> Three days before.

The beauty and delicacy of the words announcing the death of the king's mother create a unique moment. The king will react to this late and final piece of news twice. The first time, staring into space: "What! mother dead!" The second time, somewhat later, crying out as if in the grip of a dull ache: "My mother dead!" The son will follow the mother. The symmetries become almost savagely clear. Arthur's mother will also die. The two mothers and the two sons, dead. What seems extraordinary to me is that after the death of his mother, King John loses heart, he remains alone, begging for the sentimental succour that none will give him. This bond between mother and son is astonishing.

Another symmetry, meticulously developed, is revealed with an unsparingness that harrows you. At the beginning of the play, on the eve of the war, King John makes a statement that he will pay for in the end. This is what he says, and Shakespeare will not forget his words:

> France, I am burned up with inflaming wrath,
> A rage whose heat hath this condition
> That nothing can allay, nothing but blood,
> The blood, and dearest-valued blood, of France.

Not forgetting what his protagonist says, by the end Shakespeare will afflict him with a burning fever, but this time the fever is not metaphorical and will prove deadly. King John is crucified between the two fevers. The deadly fever at the end of the play is described in minute detail. The king moans as if on a pyre, ruthlessly built by the playwright:

> There is so hot a summer in my bosom,
> That all my bowels crumble up to dust:
> I am a scribbled form drawn with a pen
> Upon a parchment, and against this fire
> Do I shrink up.

Shakespeare exacts his punishment. The torment is protracted; the king dies a lingering death. He must pay for the burning wrath he declared on the battlefield with a literal fever:

> Poisoned, ill fare; dead, forsook, cast off;
> And none of you will bid the winter come,
> To thrust his icy fingers in my maw;
> Nor let my kingdom's rivers take their course
> Through my burned bosom; nor entreat the north
> To make his bleak winds kiss my parched lips,
> And comfort me with cold: I do not ask you much,
> I beg cold comfort.

I think we have here one of Shakespeare's strangest and most enigmatic plays. The play conceals a mystery. In my production of the play, I would set out from the characters' overly abundant speech. A number of times, the characters make us understand that pain is expressed in few words. More often than not, they give lengthy speeches, negotiate treaties, break them, betray their country, go back on their betrayal, forgive each other, accuse each other. It all seems random, apart from the symmetries.

I imagine a primitive ceremony. A reconstruction of the beginning of the world, a repetition of the quarrel between Cain and Abel. We are presented with a barbarous world, where no moral code applies, a world that seethes in its own horror. The characters will be dressed in animal skins and beat tom-toms. The backdrop will be blood red: "The sun's o'ercast with blood."

One being alone will come from another world. Against this savage backdrop will appear a bride of the nineteenth century, Blanche, daughter to the King of Castile. The beginning of evil will be the sacrificing of the bride. Love will scorch the world, like a parched spring. Gripped by the fury of war, the men will no longer understand the beautiful words of love. Blanche will deliver the obituary:

> What, shall our feast be kept with slaughtered men?
> Shall braying trumpets and loud churlish drums,
> Clamours of hell, be measures to our pomp?

The end of love is described at the same time as a hellish world bent on killing. Along with the symbol of the mother and child, the symbol of the bride will burn like a relentless fire. This character will not belong to the primitive age. The bride will appear surrounded by primitive weapons. When the wedding is sacrificed, the energies of evil will be unleashed. It is also strange that the king will weep after his mother's death. Once the characters realise, it will already be far too late. Their sufferings will surpass all imagination.

I think of the end of the performance, when, over the words, speeches, theories, deeds of the characters preparing a new coronation, once the tragedies have run their course without anybody being able to stop them, I would superimpose Blanche's speech:

> The sun's o'ercast with blood: fair day adieu!
> Which is the side that I must go withal?
> I am with both: each army hath a hand,
> And, in their rage, I having hold of both,
> They whirl asunder, and dismember me.

At the same time as this voiceover, I would use feedback, a faint electronic buzz that would make the audience think of today's world, of the fact that man becomes a wild beast when weapons start to decide the fate of values, values that usually shine brightly, but which collapse into rust, which taste like lye, when terrible war barks like a wild beast.

13 *Richard III*, or essay on the comforts of peace

The cruel tragedy begins with a prologue. In an astonishing soliloquy, Richard, Duke of Gloucester, describes the world in which he lives. So far as I know, few directors have set out from the world in which this strange character begins his funereal ascent. The starting point is always Richard himself, on whom the production is then built. To me, Richard's soliloquy is defining. The savage beauty of the scenario should give rise to meditation on a particular human condition.

Richard is a soldier who has become a civilian. There is a wonderful hidden meaning here. The poor unfortunate tells us about the end of the war and finds that the society into which he is trying to integrate is less than mediocre. The world is therefore unbearable because it is at peace. What does this mean? The discovery of the happiness of tender, everyday life: dancing, conversation, the exaltation of the eternal feminine, the peace of hearth and home, the never-ending dialogue between day and night, a warm river of love and tranquillity overflows, bringing with it a balance between sleep and waking.

But what becomes of the pedant who scorns such mediocrity? He revolts. A cripple, riddled with complexes, Richard regards peace as a menace. Whence Richard's crisis? Boredom, of course. A species of spleen of which he cannot cure himself. This rather common Shakespearean malady prompts the playwright to teach Richard a lesson. But the plot itself is often a wrathful pedagogical construct. Under the aegis of allegory, the tragedy of Richard will teach us to cherish the wonders of life when they are close to the heart of innocence.

A harsh mechanism is unleashed and we shudder at the apparition of a grief-stricken face, that of a mother who has lost her child in the savage, bloody game of internecine conflict. Richard cynically dismisses the image of courtly capering and brings on stage battle cries and hatred. When is man closer to his essence? The question rends the night. Man's reflexes are sharpened. Perhaps only in *Macbeth* is there so much talk of sleep and sleeplessness. The world in which Richard lives loses the peace of the heart and of dream. Bloodthirsty warriors emerge from every corner of space, demanding their right to exist.

What seems fascinating to me in Shakespeare's play is that the Duke of Gloucester, in urging men to action, does so out of a blameworthy contempt for the garden; it is in this paradox that my production will find its metaphor. For Richard, forests, the fruits of the garden, the flowers of the world, unbounded parkland become signs of a platitude that harbours something dangerous. In the performance, the closed, secret chamber will gradually come to dominate.

How might I suggest this fateful confrontation between stone walls and the seraphic garden? The set design requires the juxtaposition of contrasting elements. Richard will be a man in love with the desert and emptiness. I am amazed by the fact that he begs forgiveness. But in a way, Shakespeare cares about him and our performance should value his qualities even if they are directed toward evil. His wooing of the widowed Anne takes one's breath away. Richard wishes to be active on every front. To facilitate his rise to power he woos women, kills brothers and even children. But what is his innermost motivation?

Boredom. And it is of this boredom, of this cruel poverty of feeling, that I wish to speak. A deformed creature, Richard suffers from boredom. A terrible condition for whomever it afflicts. A modern feeling, expressed in the poetry of Baudelaire, for example. It is not important that our performance accuse, so much as it important that we explore in detail the vice afflicting the character, seeking to understand how it arose, how it found its way into a man's heart.

I very much admire *Richard III* because it is a parable of taking the wrong path. The path is suspenseful because in a world ruled by an evil genius you cannot put a foot wrong. For the slightest mistake you lose your head. What is life like in such a world? What form does the ugly take there, and what can become beautiful?

There are people who delight in a mere walk in the park, while others feel pleasure only when they witness a bloody bullfight. Richard has lost all joy in life. He craves strong sensations. He needs adventure. The web he weaves is so tangled that our performance must gradually become labyrinthine.

It will be exactly like getting lost. Whereas in the beginning, we will present a world whose musical accompaniment is the pleasing of a lute, later everything will become disquieting, hermetic, walled in. Peaceful dancers will receive burnt garments, while dazzling knights invade the stage, bursting into almost sacral spaces. We will tangle the meanings of the world, mindful of Richard's bitter mistake. I think of the cursed beauty of the Teuton knights in Eisenstein's *Alexander Nevsky*. The banality of simple gifts is replaced with demonic attractions. An evil spirit has descended from the murk and lights twisted tapers. It is the overthrow of equilibrium that captivates me in this play.

We will seek a hidden relation between the ethical and the aesthetic. Like a desert invading a forest, engulfing a garden, it will come to dominate gradually, in allegorical wise. The action will continue unabated, since the world is always on the brink. This mysterious story will end with a moral, like every fable. Richard himself will utter it: "My kingdom for a horse." This is where it all has led. The fairy-tale world imagined by Richard has a violent, unhealthy hue. Thick, unsightly, corroding rust dominates. We will then understand Richard as a murderous functionary who tries to teach Homer a lesson. The relationship between the true poetry of life and courage, on the one hand, and Richard's wretched, villainous oasis, on the other, will accompany events as an overarching theme.

Richmond comes to power after Richard. The world needs a Richmond because he restores the peace of sleep and love for the fruits of the earth.

14 The eternal Katherine.
The Taming of the Shrew

We all know the story of Katherine. We intuit that the inexorable surge of her soul has a deep source. We sympathise with her astonishing transformation. What might we say about this character who is so well written but often so superficially acted? Katherine is our very soul. In her there is such detestation of mediocrity and pettiness that we cannot help but love her with deep thoughtfulness and esteem. What might Katherine gain from her milieu, in which choice flowers have no place? Her urges come up against walls and rocks. A void, an asphyxiating lack stalks Katherine. Her sharp senses understand the barrenness, her warm heart is chilled by the mediocrity that enticingly, villainously encroaches on the very seat of life. A strong personality, Katherine furiously defends herself. Her very existence is a struggle. But the world understands nothing of the fear that floods Katherine feelings. For, this impoverished world has neither faith nor ideals nor even illusions. What can Katherine do, pent as she is in her solitude? Nothing. But here Shakespeare intervenes and pardons his heroine. He makes her encounter an enchanter.

In a way, Katherine is Cinderella. Thirsting for the beautiful in a banal, derisory world, she will only find salvation in a great love. To our century, so avid for love and at the same time so devoid of it, Katherine is a consummate symbol. We know her story, but an unquenchable thirst for joy and ritual summons us to represent her destiny. I would like to realise a performance about the power of love. I would like the play's rare and precious *je ne sais quoi* to flood our eyes and hearts. In order for it to do so, first we will need to describe Katherine's milieu. Acerbically, unsparingly.

An ordinary, insignificant provincial town harbours wealthy families who transact fortunes through arranged marriages. Katherine's sister, Bianca, is subject to this tradition. But Katherine has a reputation for shrewishness. The situation is petty, commonplace. We suffer only as long as Katherine's freedom is at stake. The stage will depict an arid space. A few household items between bare walls. Something cold and austere, uncommon to comedy. For, our performance will represent a path, a journey, in which the masks will have to fall with a certain amount of solemnity. I would go so far as to make Katherine undergo a visible and astonishing transformation. An unusual relationship between two guises. Wearing a mask at first, Katherine will change her visage as she becomes tamed. Since her taming is the very birth of her soul. In the warm flame of being esteemed, Katherine will revive. Removed from the banal and mediocre course of tradition, Katherine will reveal the treasures of a radiant heart and sensibility, which were barely perceptible at first. She desires her taming, as a proof of her originality, just as Saint-Exupéry desires the taming of the characters that surround the Little Prince.

The event must occur exactly like a miracle. And it is here that the enchanter makes his entrance. As I imagine it, Petruchio should resemble the enchanters in Fellini's films, those strange directors, those seekers of the beautiful, wandering through utterly ordinary towns, true creators of modern enchantments.

Petruchio is accompanied by numerous attendants who together make up an experimental theatre company. Wielders of a secret magic, in every town they pitch a circus big top, a wretched tent, but one that brings delight. Accompanied by wild animals, these servants of an unknown ideal will take their places and wait. A wait heavy with ripe fruit and full of burning emotion. Nothing frightens them, for they know the great torments of the world. Having passed through hell and purgatory, these enchanters bring with them the breath of celebration. What will happen in this starched, mediocre little town? With difficulty, in flame and gold, something that bears a beautiful name will arise. A soul will spread two gigantic wings, ready to touch the North Star and the Heavens. Here we find Petruchio prior to the experiment, speaking as only a well-travelled man knows how to speak:

> Think you a little din can daunt mine ears?
> Have I not in my time heard lions roar?
> Have I not heard the sea puff'd up with winds
> Rage like an angry boar chafed with sweat?
> Have I not heard great ordnance in the field,
> And heaven's artillery thunder in the skies?
> Have I not in a pitched battle heard
> Loud 'larums, neighing steeds, and trumpets' clang?
> And do you tell me of a woman's tongue,
> That gives not half so great a blow to hear
> As will a chestnut in a farmer's fire?
> Tush, tush! fear boys with bugs.

The process of Katherine's transformation will take on the aspect of a secret ritual. Experiments of the heart cannot have the appearance of something mediocre, something ordinary. It will be like in a fairy tale where the hero or heroine must cast off an unfavourable guise. Through faith and love, Katherine will rid herself of something ugly and bad. She will be reborn beneath our very eyes in a ceremony that brings radiant warmth. At the end of the play, I would like flowers to rain down on the stage. Arm in arm with Petruchio, Katherine will go from century to century like a fairy who has been restored the power to grant wishes, having emerged from out of herself and into the light.

The process of becoming, accompanied by music and strange gestures, will symbolise the eternal birth of a free soul. It will be based on a precise relationship between body and soul. The true arraying of the body, described by Shakespeare via Petruchio's dealing with the tailors, will be performed ritually. Everything will be enveloped in mystery, as if it were something difficult and cumbersome, a forging of new relationships between man and the world, between man and his fellow man. Being symbolic, the actions will pave the way to rebirth. Passing through a purgatory, Katherine will liberate her sensibility in the incandescence required by her choice and truthful soul.

15 Poetry and murder.
Titus Andronicus

How far can a man go down the unknown path of murder? The question harrows me; it is like a primal, savage obsession. Is it possible to take the dark, malevolent path of murder only by yourself or is it also possible in company? Natural questions for a man born in the twentieth century. In my innermost self, I am terrified by such questions, thinking of realities such as Auschwitz. In fact, not even the most terrifying dream can compete with the terrifying reality in all its squalor. But if Shakespeare dreams such dreams, he never goes back on his ardent love for the sacred moral code so necessary beneath the cold and distant stars. Without a doubt, Shakespeare is the embodiment of the prophet closest to our heart. And like the dreams of every prophet, Shakespeare's are terrible in their beauty. His voice in the wilderness not only signals the vanity that stalks us, but also heralds gods in human guise. We will never be able fully to measure the beauty that his texts bring. In his work there is something elusive, almost hermetic, an infiltration of mystery that time obliges us to illumine with all the matchless power of theatre.

We shudder before paeans and evil, between poetry and murder, which, progressively articulated, advance along a path of truths necessary both to man and the world around him. I am in no hurry to decipher the mystery of *Titus Andronicus*. I sense I must delay, take an indirect path. I wonder where danger lurks and where safety can be found in this weave of bloody events? A light draws me on. I suspect that a smile peeps from behind these events, it keeps watch, like the smile of the Cheshire cat in *Alice in Wonderland*.

In *Titus Andronicus*, evil is as visible as a huge block of granite, it is a palpable, solid evil, an indecipherable evil, a self-confident, self-satisfied evil. But this evil cannot be cured by any imitative staging. Above the events of the play flutters a problematic, deceptive veil. The truth is that we would not love Shakespeare so much if he were not so innocent in his cunning ploys. We all like to playact and we intuit that at bottom sublime childhood links hands with adulthood.

What takes place in *Titus Andronicus* fills me with cosmic dread. Events unfold in a conventional space, symbolising, the same as in any other theatrical story, neutral ground. But in that space, cold draughts take the breath away and an immense cold encases people in ice.

There is nothing more inimical than cold to man without shelter under the open sky. The nobility that envelops the world of *Titus Andronicus* is like a deadly winter. What takes place is irreversible. We will always wonder where this path leads, bearing the mark of a terrifying purity. I would like the delivery of the text to resemble the recitation of a psalm in the temple. This bloody, puritanical, snowbound history will unfold slowly, majestically, a ceremony foretokening exhaustion, like the wilting of a plant violently ripped up. This ceremony must convey the symbolism of a final glimmer. We have here a group of people who give up their lives without resistance. In a way, this is a law of the theatre: if you are scripted to die, then you must do so as beautifully as you can. And perhaps it is no accident that these supreme sacrifices are dictated by a text and delivery that are rhythmic, metrical. After a time, however, harmony breaks down and a rude mechanical bursts onto the scene, speaking in coarse prose. It is only then that a beam of sunlight is broken and you realise that in *Titus Andronicus* the murderers speak in verse.

It is this poetic quality of the performance that interests me above all. In my production, a highly aestheticising relationship between the action and its integument should take on the thrilling powers of a warning. Hence too the very purpose of a performance garbed in the proud mantle of profound, archetypal culture, bringing warmth to the endless winter of evil. At the same time, I think that today more than ever, shining wisely and piously, more often than not ignored, art and poetry vibrate in humility, overwhelming in their subterranean energies, in a space whose future has been thrown into doubt: old Mother Earth.

This is why my production of *Titus Andronicus* would be about not human evil but the beauty of culture, and at the same time, I would ask what could be more terrible than a mannered meeting of poetry and murder, a manner about which Jean Genet has written so disturbingly. We do not wonder that Shakespeare is a prophet, but his prophecies have a hidden meaning, whose mysteries we are sometimes duty-bound to decipher. I am convinced that rarely has the stage played host to a speech more terrible than the one spoken by Aaron, in whose words a black-blooded dragon gnashes at the air:

Lucius: Art thou not sorry for these heinous deeds?
Aaron: Ay, that I had not done a thousand more.
   Even now I curse the day (and yet, I think,
   Few come within the compass of my curse),
   Wherein I did not some notorious ill:

As kill a man, or else devise his death;
Ravish a maid, or plot the way to do it;
Accuse some innocent, and forswear myself:
Set deadly enmity between two friends;
Make poor men's cattle break their necks;
Set fire on barns and haystacks in the night,
And bid the owners quench them with their tears.
Oft have I digg'd up dead men from their graves,
And set them upright at their dear friends' doors
Even when the sorrow almost was forgot;
And on their skins, as on the bark of trees,
Have with my knife carved in Roman letters,
Let not your sorrows die, though I am dead.
Tut, I have done a thousand dreadful things,
As willingly as one would kill a fly;
And nothing grieves me heartily indeed,
But that I cannot do ten thousand more.

Despite this pestilent outpouring of evil, I conceive of an apparently inno-cent performance. What could be more overwhelming, more shocking, than a group of children who, at play, without realising it, reach the heights of savagery, utterly unconscious of the evil they do, the very unconscious-ness that forms the morally redemptive reserves of a world that needs to be reborn.

I envisage a performance with a group of child actors aged between fourteen and seventeen. The children will be garbed in the most fantastical Asiatic ceremonial costumes, brightly coloured, of the finest silk, clothing bodies that know the secret of the choicest movements and the music of the strangest hymns, coldly glinting. It will be of a penetratingly elegiac nobil-ity, close to the vague intuition of a finale whose images will be terrifyingly beautiful. The severing of Titus Andronicus's arm will be symbolised by the snapping of a blossoming branch.

Lavinia will wear strips of ruby satin for severed hands, and the frequent murders will be symbolised by the falling of masks. The banquet of death will have the ritualistic character of Mexican festivals, where candy skulls are laid on the table. The performance will have a lively, exuberant mood, an unusual gaiety, redolent of poetry, symbol, play, accompanied by songs, an unwittingly depraved party, full of killing, with smiles that may or may not be cunning hovering above it all. It will be necessary to awaken in the audience an urge to stop the ceremony, to stop the game, not to let it reach its conclusion, its terrifying end, an urge that must be felt from the very first, in the moment when the child actors dance onto the stage.

16 The city's misfortune. *Twelfth Night*

Is Illyria an enchanted realm or an insignificant city, a walled provincial town that squanders its vigour in sterile entertainments, pastimes voided of the powerlessness and misfortunes that accompany in slow motion characters low or lordly, a barren saraband conducted only by wine and insomnia? The characters of Shakespeare's Illyria are tortured by eternal waiting, a waiting sometimes vague, sometimes anxious. It is from this psychological state, the waiting that haunts every corner of the city, that my directorial meditation would set out, a meditation on the indecipherable mystery of *Twelfth Night*.

It seems highly significant to me that Illyria, the small city of Illyria, is a port on an unknown sea. We do not ignore the fact that Shakespeare suggests that military patrols continuously scour the sea and every corner of the city in search of foreigners. I sense that there is not much peace in Illyria. A menace hovers over the territory and only the cries of the drunkards interrupt the silence that reigns there day and night. A dogmatic disquietude hovers over the inhabitants of Illyria. Might it be that the mood of this seemingly exuberant but ultimately bitter comedy resembles the metaphysical condition of the garrison in Dino Buzzati's *Tartar Steppe*? An enigma coils around my mind, signalling danger. I am obsessed with the sand of the shore, which the wild wind must whip up and blow through the streets of the city.

There is something sterile about the action of *Twelfth Night*, like a dry rot that threatens the sap of a living trunk. A seemingly innocent monotony roams the city alongside the characters and is always present in their lives. A blasé duke courts an equally bored countess. Apart from this stereotypical plot, no other event colours any living screen. Lifeless ritual, words emptied of content, joyless promenades, feasts without any appetite for food: this is what happens, on the surface. And subterranean, stultifying wassails, the terrible celebrations of the ill-adapted.

If Viola did not arrive here in Illyria, then fear would certainly pervade it more menacingly, and the people would watch with growing terror the edge of the advancing desert. In fact, it is plain that the elegant Countess Olivia is slowly sinking into the sand, as if in an absurdist play by Samuel Beckett. Every character in *Twelfth Night* tries to cadge a hope that none is willing to give. The banal stereotypy of life in Illyria menaces the innermost recesses of the soul. Each of the characters, lucidly aware of their poverty of spirit, craves the slightest glimmer of hope on the horizon.

Always kind in his cruelty, Shakespeare forgives these threatened beings for a fraction of time and sends the inhabitants of the cold, almost deserted city a girl of pure heart and innocent outlook. With the power of her youth, it is Viola's destiny to attempt to break the crust of petrified ash. She tries to save these characters from imminent catastrophe. What could be more catastrophic than universal automatism, which is able to crush freedom, ideals, and hope?

In my production, Viola will arrive here in Illyria through a tunnel in time. She will be dressed in the fashion of the unknown, unremembered spaces from whence she comes. She is a vulnerable being, so delicately frail that we will feel an urge to protect her. After her arrival, things carry on as if nothing has happened, but at the same time, imperceptible changes begin to alter the age-old provincial way of life. Countess Olivia falls in love with Viola, who is disguised as a boy; the duke at last has a good friend; the drunkards wish to punish the upstart youth. But Viola brings a breath of magic, which colours the city and just when everything seems to have got back to normal, sounds of danger announce that in the meantime military preparations have been made in a world still not healed.

What parable more topical might arise from an unknown space that we watch in astonishment, waiting for truth to emerge? This world, in which boredom is the only celebration allowed, sleeps on, unable to grasp the growing menace that darkens its horizon. Shakespeare is too astute a researcher of the world not to place not only life but also death in the balance. His bitter and dark comedies arouse disquiet in us. The law of his stories says that nothing is gratuitous. We spend just eleven nights of unawareness and on the final night, the twelfth, we discover what we have not seen hitherto.

Among all these events, the fate of Malvolio seems strange to me. The joke played on Malvolio has deeper meanings. Something Dionysian takes place, something savage, a punishment too cruel not to expose an ancestral malice, which springs from the shadows of a soul that displays an acute lack of perspective. Malvolio's sufferings have their own meaning. It is something that cannot be imparted, the same as it is impossible to impart an erotic experience.

The events in the city fade away. What is left behind is like an absence, an emptiness. When at last all the characters fall into slumber, while only the fool sings in his sleep, we will understand that in the shining desert a strange phenomenon has occurred. And the story will take on tragicomic meanings having to do with people who have missed the opportunity to wake up. Swallowed by the city, Viola will follow the path of sacrifice out of too great a love for man. Her power to love will be unable to redeem the city. Just as a single flower does not mean that spring has come. While the people sleep their careless, hopeless sleep, as if in an apocalyptic lethargy, unknown soldiers conquer the secret realm of Illyria once and for all.

17 The wretchedness of psychology. *Othello*

Othello undergoes a strange process of involution. We watch the terrifying process of his fall from the snow-clad sacred heights. Over the course of the play, Othello discovers the cruel wretchedness of the Real. A hero, a warrior, the bravest of the brave, Othello gradually loses the freedom to act. In the end, he is forced to learn to inhabit a house.

The fierce, flaming battlefields, the towering waves of storm-tossed seas, the looking down on the rest of the world from the heights, all is gradually reduced to the petty events of a home. Othello discovers *walls*. The erstwhile commander of troops is appointed governor of an island at the beginning of the play. His field of action is abruptly narrowed and with a shudder of the heart he takes stock of a world that needs peace, a petty world desirous of tranquillity. From the very beginning of the tragedy we intuit an unnatural state of affairs. The road on which Othello sets out holds peril. We take the valiant hero's side and, in our hearts, we wish him greatness. But what starts to unfold is like an envenomed waft, something insinuating, an unexpressed punishment. The danger is clear, but it is announced like an inauspicious season read in the stars.

Without saying so out loud, the erstwhile warrior suddenly feels corseted. With slow and terrible gait, the tragedy proceeds. Nothing can stand in its way. Othello has been chosen by an inimical fate. We divine the destiny that takes shape around him without seeing it. The haste with which he accepts the post of governor is almost pathetic. It conceals disquiet and forebodings. But everything still seems to be held in balance. Although in this kind of situation Othello seems quite uncomfortable, in his need for calm, his acute need for equilibrium, he clings desperately to the home he has created for himself at the last moment.

His wife, the delicate Desdemona, becomes the final support for a man who, as he says, entered the world of soldiers and their terrifying wars at the age of seven. We therefore watch a restrictive process, in which Othello discovers his own poverty. What meanings are concealed herein? A man who has known great stress, glory, victories, an inveterate idealist who has travelled the continents comes into contact with something real, palpable, immediate, but which also brings with it fear. He who has never been afraid, not even of the furious ocean or the desert.

I experience as a dramatic sign the fact that once Othello arrives on the island the coffers of his wealth are unloaded and taken to the house where he will live. It is something domestic and petty. He is shadowed by the train of the possessions he has accumulated over a lifetime. They are real, but hideous, and they slither behind him like a snake. What do the coffers unloaded from the admiral's ship contain? Without doubt, petty, insignificant objects. Souvenirs of his passage through the vast and savage world. We fear for our hero. Such preparations for habitation are so hasty, so unnatural. . . .

I cannot help but think of Citizen Kane's huge crematorium in the Orson Welles film, where, at the end of his life, the protagonist burns all his possessions. At one point, a childhood sledge appears, terrible in its innocence. The valiant Othello is preparing to settle down. He feels threatened and, in his desperation, he wishes to defend his final haven, the island and his wife.

But now a strange, indecipherable figure appears. Iago. He is first of all a highly subtle psychologist. He intuits Othello's situation at a single glance and divines how fragile is his position, how precarious is the equilibrium. "I am not what I am," says Iago, and we shudder to hear him, to behold him. A petty servant, without any great desire for advancement, Iago has a restlessness about him, something that gleams coldly, like quicksilver, something that conceals an indeterminate depth, a danger so great that it fills us with terror to see him go about his business so calmly.

I imagine Iago as like the petty functionary who visits Adrian Leverkühn in Thomas Mann's *Doktor Faustus*. Iago should have the same baggy trousers, checked jacket, and loud necktie. Mefisto moves within his being, glinting coldly. Othello says that if he ceased to love, he would succumb to chaos. A lover of disorder, of dark entropies, with scholarly refinement and emotionless calm, Mefisto creates a chasm for him who clings to love as his final support. Iago is so inhuman in his pedantry and makes such perfect use of his knowledge of the deepest reaches of the human soul that he becomes the most dreadful character in all of Shakespeare.

The calculated destruction of Othello unfolds within a space that is unspectacular and devoid of any martial valour. My production would be cold rather than hot, consisting of the gradual discovery of pettiness, of the most banal reality. A performance in which the great Othello discovers his dwelling place. A castle with long halls and dark doorways, full of alien objects, a reality that repulses the protagonist. At night, I even dream of the walls of Othello's castle.

The walls are grey, grubby, tinged green in places. Just how petty and degrading is Othello's psychological development, skilfully, malevolently guided by Iago, becomes evident in the evidence of the handkerchief. This insignificant item slays Desdemona. The link between a rabid, seething unconscious and a consciousness gradually lulled to sleep is skilfully forged by the toxic psychologist.

In the final scene, Othello's troubled gaze sees alien people around him, unfamiliar objects, rust, filthy colours, a world so wretched, so decayed that not even suicide can save him from this mire of sensorial degradation. Othello's story is the drama of a man overwhelmed by the wretchedness of a reality. He who ought to have been borne aloft on the wings of legend comes crashing down, broken by the ugly, unworthy effects of a psychology as violent as it is impoverished: the psychology of jealousy. Let us shudder at the lucid lament of the protagonist stalked by darkness:

> Farewell the tranquil mind! Farewell content!
> Farewell the plumed troop, and the big wars,
> That make ambition virtue! O, farewell!
> Farewell the neighing steed, and the shrill trump,
> The spirit-stirring drum, the ear-piercing fife,
> The royal banner; and all quality,
> Pride, pomp, and circumstance of glorious war!
> And O, you mortal engines, whose rude throats
> The immortal Jove's dread clamours counterfeit,
> Farewell! Othello's occupation's gone!

18 The servants of night.
Macbeth

That Macbeth is afraid of the light is well known. Almost his every action is crowned with darkness. His deeds take place at night. Macbeth desires concealment. He does not want to be seen by anybody as he breaks every human law. For, Macbeth heeds no law. A hardened killer, he moves from murder to murder.

> I am in blood
> Stepp'd in so far that should I wade no more
> Returning were as tedious as go o'er.

A cruel tyrant, Macbeth surrounds himself with other murderers. He is supported psychologically by his wife. Both desire his advancement. But in addition to their obsession with grandeur, they also desire joy. But this they cannot have. It cannot be said that this royal couple do not preserve a final vestige of wisdom. But they have no richness of soul. In vain do we seek it in their deeds. An asphyxiating darkness clings to their characters and deeds like a stench. Macbeth and his wife remain at the savage, primitive level of murder. There is not one glimmer of equilibrium. When threatened, they want to drag the whole of mankind down with them into the abyss. Macbeth's conjuration of the witches bears witness to this:

> Though you untie the winds, and let them fight
> Against the churches; though the yesty waves
> Confound and swallow navigation up;
> Though bladed corn be lodged and trees blown down;
> Though castles topple on their warders' heads;
> Though palaces and pyramids do slope
> Their heads to their foundations; though the treasure
> Of nature's germens tumble all together,
> Even till destruction sicken; answer me
> To what I ask you.

What might one say about such an attitude? If Macbeth had an atomic bomb, he would destroy the rest of the world with him when he met his end. What is the meaning of this cruel tragedy? In my opinion, Macbeth embodies not only a ferocious murderer, but also a psychology without equal in its baseness. When Richard III unleashed the terrifying machinery of dictatorship, he did so with a certain strange, secret personal charm. At the height of the horror, he had the seductiveness of a glittering snake. A certain cold, dangerous attraction went hand in hand with his demonic nature, winning a certain naïve trust on the part of others.

But the character of Macbeth relates to a dark, subterranean world. Macbeth is gloomy, coarse, bestial. Awkward, without a trace of wit, his mind works like tumbling boulders crushing all in their path. Grace enrages him, causes him to seethe with vindictive envy. There is so much futility in him, such a lack of quality, that this monster can only arouse contempt. Stepping into the arena of history, Macbeth brings with him such primitivism, such darkness that even nature loses patience.

> The night has been unruly: where we lay,
> Our chimneys were blown down and, as they say,
> Lamentings heard i' the air, strange screams of death,
> And prophesying, with accents terrible,
> Of dire combustion and confused events
> New hatch'd to the woeful time: the obscure bird
> Clamour'd the livelong night: some say, the earth
> Was feverous and did shake.

Macbeth does not know how to dissemble and this is why he is capable only of killing, thinking that at the end of his serial killings much-craved peace might lie. It is strange that both he and his wife lose their minds on the dark path they take. They have mental breakdowns. Alone and unhappy, their striving for a peaceful haven seems hideous to us. With subtlety and refinement, Shakespeare exhaustively details this type of personality, warning us of the dangers it brings. What is the meaning of the witches in this context? I think that these corrupt soothsayers represent the hidden, disordered face of Macbeth's 'I.'

My production, which would focus on detailed psychological analysis, would metaphorically open up Macbeth's self. Viscerally depicted, his 'I' would be like a body with its innards cruelly laid bare. His self would resemble the circuitry of a robot. In Macbeth I see a Polyphemus, a terrifying cyclops. Clinical analysis of disproportionately evil deeds juxtaposed with the delicate scale of the human would veer off in the direction of fantastical. Rabid grandiloquence contrasting with the peace of the world would provide the meditative antithesis of a harsh performance. With every murder, Macbeth hypertrophies, finally becoming an ogre whose heads must be cut off. The assemblies of fugitives from his land will resemble councils of the wise and fair.

Macbeth is cumbersome in his thinking. From him have fled joy, music, and poetry. Grace is alien to him. Encased in chainmail, he becomes more and more impotent. His philosophy reveals him to us as a creature who understands nothing of life:

> Out, out, brief candle!
> Life's but a walking shadow, a poor player
> That struts and frets his hour upon the stage
> And then is heard no more: it is a tale
> Told by an idiot, full of sound and fury,
> Signifying nothing.

Nothing can protect Macbeth from the fury of the wronged. The immense cold that surrounds him, the night and evil that seethe within him make us see his end as the slaying of a cruel ogre, whose decapitated body spurts dark, foul-smelling blood. *Macbeth*, like Jarry's *Ubu Roi*, describes the hypertrophied paranoia of a dictator.

19 *Hamlet*

Hamlet's silences annoy me, as does his slow discursiveness. In our hurried century, such a character gets on your nerves. Hamlet analyses at length, without being able to act. Why? Herein lies the mystery of Shakespeare's masterpiece. To answer the question seems to be the whole purpose of a directorial interpretation. How delightful to be an intrepid interpreter of the play! For, the truth is that you need courage to approach the terrible secrets of the Danish prince.

I feel within me a terrible joy, waves of warm emotion. I feel happy reading this tragedy, cruel in its plot, but enveloped in a nimbus, an aureole that can only be the sign of its sublime genius. As one unravels the words and action, the mysterious power of the Theatre comes to life, garbed in a robe of diamond and flame. We are obliged to examine, carefully and soberly, the hidden structure, radiant in its meanings. We will be spiritually enriched thereby, and our artistic endeavours will be lent hope and impetus. Via *Hamlet* we will find ourselves at the heart of the Theatre, at the seething core of life and death. We will toil to analyse the mystery, employing thoroughness and patience. Let our toil be rewarded by discovery of the truth in the enacted words and the unspoken deeds.

Reading *Hamlet*, you do not have the same sensation as when you see a performance of the text. Reading the play is difficult, it demands that you keep going back, rereading the text to see the connections between word and potential deed; that you try to understand it, to seek its meaning. The hope that accompanies you when you read the play is different than your emotion on watching the construct of a performance as it relentlessly unfolds. In any event, when you read it, major difficulties arise, stumbling blocks in the path of the imagination, the cruel stereotypy of the already known. What is necessary is a small enigma, a secret to reading so that the structure might begin to live through you. Before embarking on the winding road of my imaginary performance, I would like to understand the characters, their personalities, their attitudes. Let me pretend that I do not know what the play is about; let me try to make innocent first contact with the grim cast. And I shall begin with the exasperating Prince of Denmark.

The life of Prince Hamlet unfolds in a tribal context. We are dealing with events typical of the political power struggle. In a typically Shakespearean setting, a young prince here attempts to fathom life and human relations.

Shakespeare creates the character of the young prince with great subtlety, while at the same time deploring him. As ever, the playwright remains objective. It is more than clear that Shakespeare does not take the side of any particular character, but rather he distantly depicts exemplary actions. It is a dramaturgical lesson that the director must absorb. An adept of the distancing effect, I cannot "take Hamlet's side." I strive to create my own critical viewpoint of him. It depends on my own sensibility. I have a secret, almost whispering sense of Shakespeare's callousness. He has no tears for the Prince of Denmark, only cruel smiles. So many mistakes are unforgivable. For, Hamlet is unable to escape his context, but remains an industrious representative of the ills that have invaded the polity. With every scene of the unfolding drama, Hamlet becomes more blameworthy. Laden with sins, he gives up the ghost without us being certain that his spirit has obtained the state of grace that each of us craves. It is this attitude that lies at the base of my directorial construct. And I am content, as if having discovered an unknown code. The dramatic lesson Hamlet is taught by life becomes learning itself, pure pedagogy. I am sensitive to the venom on Hamlet's breath and I cannot help but tremble as I imagine the malice that gives rise to evil. For, there is no good to be found anywhere in the castle where the tragedy unfolds. A directorial viewpoint that requires *distancing* makes me inclined to plumb the depths of an all-too-familiar magical construct.

I might name Hamlet Prince Spleen. It is acknowledged that he suffers from terrible boredom. That life has lost its charm for him. Obsessed with the evil within him and around him, he is capable of thinking of nothing but revenge. But he delays out of a lack of energy. Lost in vain dreams, his actions become more and more flaccid. Like a fairy-tale prince obsessed forevermore with slaying the dragon, he is incapable of protecting the one crumb of life and love a man needs in order to survive. Hamlet roams the deserted castle arm in arm with Lady Death. Garbed in black, the aged Lady Death smiles her self-confident smile.

Hamlet becomes a slave of finitude. Incapable of bringing light or saving what might still be saved, he desires the end with all his tortured soul. In the name of death, he bears with him a curse. It is natural that all the characters be afraid of his presence. The dark, misfortune-bearing prince is a stranger to joy. He is obsessed with slaking a vast need, for which he pines funereally. His body is enveloped in a terrifying nimbus, the outward sign of the cold and emptiness in his soul. In the final act, there is a scene that takes place in a graveyard. The Prince of Denmark feels at ease there. With great curiosity, he inspects the sacred ground, the final threshold. In my production, the betrothal to death that Hamlet cultivates will become the overriding metaphor. Afflicted by moods of desolation, Hamlet will resemble a Luciferian demon.

As an art lover, with the players Hamlet conceives a performance that he intends to be terrifying. A play within the play. The kind of performance Hamlet imagines will therefore be of interest. He becomes the conductor of a ritual or, in contemporary terms, a director. The artistic means he employs, the style of the show he creates, become important. We have an opportunity to stage an essay about the theatre and the art of direction. I picture the young prince garbed in a dark mantle, working with the actors on their stage gestures, on their diction, on the aesthetics of the theatrical performance. Here, the director is the chosen one.

But what kind of performance would Hamlet put on? One in which actors dressed in black gaze menacingly, acting their parts in the shadow, almost in darkness. It is in this performance that the mystery and essence of Hamlet's destiny lies. It is his only grounded act, his only joy, albeit one darkened by the thought of revenge. Hamlet does not understand art as a joy in the desert of life. The curse he bears with him acts on his implacable destiny like a blunt instrument. How might we save Hamlet? We cannot. The old lady, Death, kissed him on the lips while he was yet in the cradle, kindling in his tender soul a strangely glinting, cold flame. The tragedy depicts the torture of this unhappy youth who, as Nietzsche says, has gazed into the abyss of existence, thereby losing any sense of the meaning of things and the ability to act. Hamlet is incapable of giving life any other meaning than that contained within his almost insane obsession. He symbolises what has been called "absurd man."

Hamlet finds no meaning to life and wonders whether or not it is worth living. "To be or not to be," this is his dilemma: I don't know whether anything can be likened to this contempt for the delicacy of existence; the brutal question is an agonised moan. The thought of death hovers over the castle. Like a teenage punk, Hamlet slouches along dark corridors, nurturing his cosmic rage. He cannot be helped. His solitude is his poison and his drug. Hamlet doesn't do dialogue. He talks to himself. Shackled to his secret, it is impossible for him to strike up any relationship. Given the secret, everybody else becomes problematic. Horatio is far too mediocre to be able to help him. Hamlet's path is convoluted, but it will finally lead to revenge. Events gain momentum and he who must die dies, but without Hamlet being able to rejoice in justice being done, since he too dies. The nightmare ends, but we are filled with grief. The wretchedness of the Real rudely barges into the midst of the action. The dream solidifies into the drabness of physical symptoms: the wounded Hamlet experiences the physiology of poisoning.

Sweat, dizziness, nausea. Bluntly woken from the dream, from pure thought, his eyes bulging in fright, his breath laboured, he sees for the first time the hideous faces, the unsightly physical reality. Hamlet dies a nasty death. His nausea outlives him. The performance should gradually acquire a striking palpability. The hideousness that colours the nooks and crannies, the faces, should become more and more blatant. The drowned Ophelia cannot outwardly preserve her delicate grace. A drowned body becomes hideously distorted. The palpable dross that engulfs everything will point to an understanding of the Real. The dreaming prince will learn a bitter lesson. With a shudder, we will solve the mystery of the journey from the fantastical apparition of a psychedelic ghost to the hideousness and decrepitude of a wretched, badly made world. The story of Hamlet will thereby become a colossal metaphor for the discovery of the Real.

I wholeheartedly believe in the need to stage this dramatic text. But under the influence of the vernal season that is coming to birth inside and outside me as I write, I yearn for a festive, outdoor performance. I would like my production to protect the young soul of the spectator from the insidious poison of the text. My production would be performed at dusk, on a hot summer's day, in a huge plaza, on a bare wooden stage with all the spotlights on view.

Stagehands would hurry across the stage to position the props; set designers and assistant directors would give the final instructions just before the performance; the actors would get into costume in view of the audience. . . . The honesty of this effect soothes you; it rejoices the soul. The evil would be tamed by the magic of the theatrical effect. The festiveness of it fills the heart with a vital joy. We will then feel compassion and greater understanding for the young prince so devoid of love. And we will be saddened by his fatal error, when he so savagely rejects Ophelia. Perhaps it is Spring that speaks through my words, but let it utter its hymn of rebirth, its inducement to universal love. And let us listen to the most beautiful words in the whole of the tragedy, which are whispered sweetly, timidly, by none other than the eternal Ophelia:

> O, what a noble mind is here o'erthrown!
> The courtier's, soldier's, scholar's eye, tongue, sword,
> Th'expectancy and rose of the fair state,
> The glass of fashion and the mould of form,
> Th'observed of all observers, quite, quite down!
> And I, of ladies most deject and wretched,
> That sucked the honey of his music vows,

Now see the noble and most sovereign reason
Like sweet bells jangled, out of time and harsh,
The unmatched form and feature of blown youth
Blasted with ecstasy. O, woe is me
T'have seen what I have seen, see what I see!

At dusk, on a hot summer's day, when my possible performance will be acted, I will be there, in that vast plaza, in front of the sacred stage of the Theatre, to affirm with all my being the unshakeable belief in the genius of Shakespeare and in the infinite powers of the Theatrical Art.

Figure 19.1 Twelfth Night staged by Auerliu Manea in 1975 at The National Theatre
of Cluj in Romania

Part two

Confessions

20 Confessions

The works of Shakespeare are like a huge block of ice hidden within which are hot springs. In fact, every major dramatic text has something apparently cold about it. People aren't in the habit of reading plays. Plays are receptacles of unknown signs. Ordinary reading is unsatisfactory. Herein resides the mystery of this great art: the Theatre.

Like a layer of snow, the words written by a playwright conceal future fruits. And it is theatre people who, drawing on their own warmth, expend sacred energies to drive away the cold of appearances. When the stage lights come on, a torrid summer envelops the souls of those gathered for the Rite. The Art of Theatre is the very sign of man's eternity on earth. Every evening, the words and actions have something new about them. Perhaps weariness, perhaps joy. Eyes dance joyfully. Life is born from the effervescence. The wings of thought, of the word, glitter brightly. How much beauty there is in this exchange between death and life. For, on the evening of the performance, a heavy tribute is paid. It is not easy to embody King Lear. The greatness of Paul Scofield was so obvious in a Royal Shakespeare Company performance that the actor accompanied Shakespeare unerringly. I don't wish to shock, but a dramatic text brings with it a certain quantum of death. The actor, that god of the contemporary world, pays a heavy tribute of breath and heartbeats attuned to the hidden, profound, terrible, unknown, strange psychologies of the Character. The directors, scenographers, properties people, musicians, technicians, electricians, the whole bustling world of the theatre on the night of the performance, is set in motion by a warm and human message. What an extraordinary expenditure of life for the sake of life!

When it's raining and cold outside, a depressed man withdraws into reading a soothing book. But the joy of being with your fellow man when it's cold and raining manifests itself differently: "Hurry up or we'll miss the play!" What peace on the evening of a wonderful play! Coming home, you bring with you the fantastical sensation of a sign witnessed collectively, of a vast metaphor; you are overjoyed that you have lent meaning to the world.

As long as there is peace on earth, the Theatre will be the sacred space where the cosmic lesson of love is taught, where the mysteries of unageing youth and deathless life are unravelled.

In the Director there reside impulses which, once expressed, ebb from the soul like a wave. Some repress such impulses, others cling to them. Fortunate is he who can construct a performance employing the coldness of a computer! He will objectively record desires, attitudes, reflexes, and seek to convince his actors to follow him down a wild or a tame but still objectivised road. Sometimes I would like the stage to burn in the furnace of a sentimental impulse. Sometimes I would like there to be a drizzle of dead leaves. How beautiful is the Theatre when from above the stage the properties man rains down confetti in imitation of a splendid snowfall.

But this is a season that has vanished from the stage: WINTER.
May you suffer a dry cold, you who do not believe in seasons!

In their own way, theatre people comprise a flight safety crew. For, in my opinion, a theatrical performance resembles a mission into space. The mission will be the more wonderful the closer it comes to the stars. It is true that we do not always grasp that the sky above us is starry. But this is why there is art, in order to reveal such truths. I do not believe in any theatre company that does not also meditate on the essence of the Sun. Sometimes the truth is dragged through the dust, but there will always be somebody to lift it up, to raise it to the light. How necessary is such a belief in the virtue of altitude! Light, in which the human gaze is lent a definite meaning, comprises a diaphanous garb for the actor's body. How much ecstasy in ceremonies imbued with the power of light! Should we not then attempt the disquiet of flight in our performances? In order to do so, a large group of people put together a kind of flying machine. The carpenters are busy in the workshops; the tailors make costumes evocative of mystery; strange objects are crafted; the electricians adjust the intensity of spotlights hidden from view; the set designers attempt magical nuances of colour; the technical directors, as specialised and confident as flight controllers, give curt orders through microphones. Everything is abuzz so that on opening night the grandeur of the Actor will be housed in a fixed and precise structure like quicksilver in the dial of an instrument. It is then, in the night, shot through with rays of light, that each unknown force of the Theatre will awaken to life. Such marvellous missions take your breath away. From every area of the stage and auditorium, the Actor is lent a meaning so lambent that it makes you thrill.

At every opening night, I am disturbed by feelings of uncertainty. Above all, I am afraid. I am afraid lest an accident happen. Lest the Kerkaporta of Byzantium reoccur: the gate left open, the tragic oversight that decided the fate of so mighty a city. But I always calm myself. It is true that on opening night there is nothing else a director can do. He is no different than the humblest member of the audience. He is like a child who listens to a story and is overjoyed because he recognises it. The disappearance of the director has its own charm. He senses that the spaceship is sound and, breathing a sigh of relief, he bears awestruck witness to the sacral rite of those gods, the Actors. At the end of the performance, he too will applaud the ceremonial art of people for whom it is worth living in order to follow them from one role to another and through them to read, as Hamlet says, the abstract and brief chronicles of the time.

I often think of the directors of my generation. I excitedly follow their successes and for each and every one of them I harbour thoughts of love and admiration. Each of them is a steadfast creator, brimming with creative juices. They are fanatics who, for the love of their fellow man, sacrifice themselves to the Theatre.

How refined, how astonishing, how incomparable is the art of Cătălina Buzoianu! I admire the noble isolation of Nicolae Scarlat. I am enchanted by the enthusiasms and originality of Alexandru Tocilescu. The daring and power of Alexa Visarion are unique. The cerebral dazzle of Dan Micu is his conquest of himself. Ioan Ieremia's ambitions give me courage.

They are young and will remain forever young, since in them there is a love of their fellow man so great that their message, once conveyed to the world, burns away the slag of existence and illumines its treasures. They are all authentic children, full of imagination and faith. What would we do without the feverishness they elicit all around them? Without their fears, without their insomnias? Without the terrible aura of their courage? How mediocre everything would be! How drab and fusty! What would we do without Toca to set underway yet another expedition to unknown lands? I wish always to witness Cătălina Buzoianu's dreams, as translucent and beautiful as the music of Mozart.

It is not possible to live without the beauty of this joint directorial phenomenon. Otherwise we would be stalked by the evil shadow of deadening theatrical correctness. We need the seething youth of these Romanian directors, who elevate the art of direction to the summits of an enchanting Olympus.

Often a director is overwhelmed by fear or, more accurately, terror. What is the fear that thrills the soul of a director? For whoever has seen Fellini's *8 1/2* the question becomes clearer. As the Italian director shows us, an onerous test always weighs upon us: to construct—it becomes the toil of an architecture of the Imponderable. We quake to our very depths. The bare bones of the set harrow our souls. The frivolous costumes put bags beneath our weary eyes. The rationality of the discourse makes us bleed. Where is the shore? Where are the *mysteries*? They can be glimpsed in the distance, like a looming cyclone. A struggle, a torment unacknowledged by those who write about directors, haunts our nights. Insomnias gape like wounds! But through stubborn determination we finally attain peace—the peace of the Grandeur of the Performance.

Every performance is situated between life and death. As long as you are working, the vital impulses are operative, meeting spiritual needs. But when some time has passed since you worked, something proves to be wrong. Like a painter or writer, you create without being closely bound to an institution. On the contrary, isolation becomes auspicious. But what do you do in a theatre, where you have to be cast as an actor but are not? You feel a chill seep into your body and soul. What are you living for? Where is your meaning?

I am not joking when I say that an actor who does not work grows fat, his eyes cloud, he risks becoming insensitive not only to nuances but even to strong stimuli. I realised this truth working with people who had not appeared on stage for a long time. You cease to exist. Your meaning perishes. It is then that you think of non-being. I cannot but quote from a book by Nicolae Balotă, who cites ninth-century monk Fredugisius's *On Nothing and Shadows*: "Non-being is something so empty and terrible that no amount of tears would be enough to shed over such a sad condition."

Late one night, after rehearsing with the actors from Sibiu Theatre, I went home to bed, tired, dissatisfied. Saint-Exupery says that only sleep can repair a failure. I fell asleep and was dreaming of purple butterflies when all of a sudden somebody knocked on my window from the street outside. Half-asleep, I turned on the light and outside the window I saw the familiar faces of my actors. "Don't be alarmed," they said, "but we'd like to ask you to come with us to the theatre. There's something in our performance that's not right." Today, after eighteen years of theatre, that occurrence seems to belong to the realm of the fantastic. Actors wake a director from his sleep at one o'clock in the morning because something doesn't sound right in the play: it is like some happening from a beautiful story from the olden days. Sleep and laziness often haunt our sanctuaries.

But either by himself or aided by others, the director must always awake from his sleep. it is necessary to wake up even if you are groggy with exhaustion. We must wake from our sleep, our daily sleep. The director keeps vigil over the mysterious rite of the performance. In regard to the power of waking, I remember what a friend of mine once said, a set designer who is now far away: in every performance it's possible to detect how many cups of coffee the director drank. The rest is wakefulness!

Theatre is an art of human solidarity. Perhaps nowhere else does a human collective become so united, so closely bound together, during the course of the labour of artistic embodiment. Human sensibilities, so fragile, are brought into alignment, almost like a musical harmony. When things go well, a wonderful tranquillity embraces the collective. Every person in the team is treasured and understood. Words and actions, the ritual in itself, everything makes the actors look in each other's eyes. And it is only then that you understand, with an ache in your soul, how beautiful it is when people act together. When acting is grave in its resonances, every instance of suggestiveness is greeted with applause. And when an actor falls ill, the whole team suffers. On a day when an actor does not come to rehearsals and everybody goes home sad, the walls of the theatre, the corridors, the dressing rooms, everything becomes dreary and so concrete that it frightens you. When the premiere takes place and you part with the actors, for a long time you are not cured of a certain ache of the soul, which is greater or lesser, depending on your capacity to love.

Like many others, I think that an actor has the right to be called a creator. I wonder why a painter, a writer, or a musician has the right to creative meditation, but not an actor. A theatre rehearsal has no other role than to awaken an impulse in an actor. He will go home and, resting or going for a walk, watching a film or fishing, playing tennis or listening to music, the impulse will establish an empire of reactions in his soul. For the rest of the day, the actor will be the absolute ruler of creation. Actors given the sacred right to think will come up with astonishing solutions. This is what explains record times for putting a performance on stage (Seneca's *Medea*—two weeks; Strindberg's *Miss Julia*—seven days; Tudor Mușatescu's *Titanic Waltz*—ten days).

True, I achieved these performances in record time, but mostly without being understood by everybody who responded to the production. The method of working quickly entails an accord with well-honed actors. You have to know what you want and above all to know how to create the enthusiasm that animates a collective that has set out with you on the terrible race. Actors don't like you to torture them by seeking over-cumbersome meanings and images. A theatre rehearsal should be a kind of celebration. And then, for the sake of efficiency, you have to pay attention to how quickly time passes. Take me, for example: on my way to rehearsals, I always recite to myself a quatrain by Goethe, quoted by Thomas Mann in an essay, in which Goethe glorifies the *minute*:

The hour has sixty minutes,
More than a thousand a day,
My son, forget not this fact,
And you will go a long way.

I think no further commentary is necessary.

Today, in the final decades of this century convulsed by light and shadow, by pinnacles and abysses, people go to the theatre not only to watch a famous play with great actors, but also to be witness to a reading on the part of the director. The director is a recent invention, but I think that without him the Theatre would be like the desert from which we all flee. Master of the performance, sovereign of the Theatrical Art, he oversees all the compartments of the stage like a conductor who lends his emphases to a symphony. It is true that we watch with baited breath the marvellous acting, but unless he is conducted, the actor gropes in the dark. I view the fate of the theatre as being bound to the artistic destiny of the union between a theatre company and a director.

The director is an ideologue. Outside the mysterious powers of the performance, he also paves a way to knowledge. He is the one who proposes a psycho-philosophical journey. From one play to the next, the company attains greater and greater perfection, while at the same time creating an initiatory relationship with the audience. Not only does the director propose a repertoire, but also, he takes care to place within an aura the moral model that he fanatically pursues.

Every theatrical company proposes an ethical code. For us lucid members of the new order, the theatre's educational side is highly important. Our heroes, whom we cause to live exemplary lives, come from life and from among words, but are so necessary to our historical mission that the theatrical act becomes as sacred as the wheat of the earth.

Pursuing an educative relationship with the general public, the director, being a wise teacher, is also concerned with his company of actors. He has to renew the forms of performance and in order to do so he will prepare his actors to encounter new psychological substances, which will move people's souls, rationally and viscerally. I can see no comparison closer to the truth than that between director and conductor. In any event, if we are at a concert, we are immediately interested in who is conducting. It has become the same with the Theatrical Art. We are not uninterested in who directed the latest *Macbeth*.

In the cultural history of this century, the major landmarks of stage performance remain bound to the major names in directing: Meyerhold, Vahtangov, Tairov, Craig, Peter Brook, Jerzy Grotowski, Eugenio Barba, Jean Vilar, Franco Zeffirelli. Both ideologue and pedagogue, the director has before him a vast territory waiting to be revealed, like unexplored lands. This is in order to make life and art more beautiful, ardently summoning the public to the unbridled or reticent festivals of an art that is beyond compare, so alive, so wise is its fate.

I would like to evolve together with a group of actors. Unfortunately, the conditions required for such a creative evolution are nowhere to be found. We move from theatre to theatre in search of the Grail and maybe such peregrinations trace a sacred labyrinth, which we will unravel and illuminate through our love of mankind and the theatre.

I sometimes wish to verify my opinions about the Theatre. I go to critic Valentin Silvestru, I read his weekly column in *România Literară*, the wonderful books he writes, I talk to him on the telephone. I consider him to be the foremost critic in the sacred field of the Theatre. In the critical discourse, what is always revealed in particular is not only the competence but also the capacity for artistic flight on the part of the person passing judgement. Valentin Silvestru is not only a refined proponent of theatre criticism, he is also the Architect. He will represent us to posterity after we are gone. The future keeps watch in his pen. His lofty mission is accompanied by a mysterious officiation of the theatrical act. When he attends a premiere, Valentin Silvestru not only understand the festive, ritual purpose of the occasion, but also accepts the convention brilliantly embodying the important role of the critic who keeps watch over the future meaning of the theatrical life.

In my life I have had a number of astonishing opportunities. I might even say that destiny has made itself known to me in beautiful guises. Perhaps the most beautiful event was occasioned by my encounter with a wise man by the name of Liviu Ciulei. He has displayed his innate brilliance as a director both here in Romania and abroad. I am moved when I think of this unique magician of the Theatrical Art. Liviu Ciulei is one of the foremost names in Contemporary Theatre. Nobody today deems it unnatural to place the Romanian director alongside Peter Brook, or Zefirelli, or Strehler. How did Liviu Ciulei learn to enchant us so powerfully? What were the secrets he learned when he was initiated into the mysteries of the stage? When I saw Liviu Ciulei for the first time in my life, I was so shocked by his gaze that to this day I cannot forget the warmth and fascinating brilliance of his eyes.

Whenever Liviu Ciulei entered the theatre on Strada Schitu Măgăreanu, before anything else he would take his hat off and move forward full of emotion. I understood that the Lucia Sturdza Bulandra Theatre was a temple, and its director a fervent priest. How many times I have wept or laughed watching plays directed by Liviu Ciulei! Powerful, emotive plays, which trouble and elevate the soul. From him I learned that in theatre you must love mankind above all else.

For whoever has seen his *Moments of Life*, based on Saroyan, it is obvious where Ciulei learned the mysteries of the theatre. Ciulei was not a member of any secret theatre academy. No! His inspiration, warmth, imagination derive from his love of man. This is how an authentic artist becomes a great director. May his sixty years bring him yet further fantastical strength to create, for Liviu Ciulei's successes are successes of the Romanian theatre.

An empty theatre auditorium in semi-darkness makes you shudder. There is something funereal about it. When a service light is burning on stage, casting its dry illumination over the auditorium, it gives you a chill. But what a difference between the desolation of the auditorium and the large number of people who gather for an opening night. It is then that you realise the beauty of human communion. So many hearts beating together, so many eyes moist with emotion. It is fascinating. About this feeling, I have written a one-act play, an essay about the theatre, which is called *Theatre Rehearsal*. At one point, a student discovers an empty theatre auditorium. Her soliloquy is as follows:

I come from afar. I have travelled a thousand and one nights by train. I am weary and pale. Something tells me that a great secret, a great mystery awaits me here. Look! Wildflowers have begun to grow on the old boards of the stage. An oak grows with sturdy branches from the prompter's box. These are the signs of a major change in the theatre. It is a time that is giving way to another time. I might say that a transformation is taking place. One generation departs and another arrives. A new theatrical spring is beginning. Long have I waited in the cold damp auditoriums of the Institute for this spring. Many nights have I dreamed, under the harsh boarding school blanket, of this flower meadow. One night this very primrose I see here appeared to me in a dream. If a river flowed here I would bathe naked in it to gain strength. In the auditorium I see not one spectator. It is dark. I am afraid. An old director is asleep in a meadow full of flowers. I am afraid. I don't like it. It's cold. There are no people. When the actors rehearse in a theatre without spectators, Death steals into their ritual. I will do something to attract an audience. Let the people come! Let the people come! (*She takes a drum*) People!

People! Soon the great performance will begin. Soon you will see what has never been seen! Roll up! Roll up! People! People! Aeschylus and Shakespeare await you within, let the performance begin. Roll up! Roll up! (*People gather in the auditorium*)

The student's words express the fear of the empty auditorium. Every theatre person treasures the performance, the shared, human celebration of a meaning. Coming to the theatre, people respect the grandeur of Theatre and with the actors they unravel the mysteries of life, of the moment, of eternity. We theatre people are ready to applaud the audience who, by coming to the show, preserve in their hearts faith in the priceless values of the Theatrical Art.

I remember with amusement that seven years ago, when I was a director at the State Theatre in Turda, overwhelmed by depression and exhaustion, I tried to rid myself of that negative mood by writing a short story about a director. The short story was simply called *The Director*. It was the story of an adolescent who has run away from home, seeking a small theatre where, together with a small group of people, he might dedicate himself to love and the Theatrical Art. The story ends tragically, when the theatre where the young man is rehearsing collapses and the stage is swallowed by the abyss. It was couched in surrealistic language, replete with fantastical happenings.

   During his wanderings, the young director is affianced to a set designer, and together they encounter the theatre that awaits them in a small town that I named simply K. Since I have just been talking about the student from the Theatre Institute, I shall now reproduce, preserving my sense of humour, the arrival of the two lovers in that small town. The chapter of the novella was called "The Station of the Small Town."

   The brass band twice intoned the triumphal march to welcome the two lovers. They were holding hands. In the middle of the station, a fountain lit by coloured light bulbs cascaded over a bride dressed in violet. The theatre director was smoking a cigarette and gazed at them confidently. After the din died away, he invited the two to board a carriage with yellow flowers and said, "Come with me, my children. I will be your father, I will make your theatrical wishes come true. I will help you to create the performance of the century." They boarded the carriage. They noticed that it had no horses. "How will we reach the town?" Maria asked. "Herein resides the enigma of our little town's station," said the director. It should be noted that you could leave that station only after midnight. The two lovers stretched out on pillows and were carried away by a sweet sleep. The director got out of the carriage and the bride dressed in violet climbed aboard in his place. Seven brides dressed in white were harnessed to the carriage. Slowly, slowly, the two softly departed, borne along by dream and the seven maidens dressed in white, heading for the small theatre of the unknown town.

It was timidly that I drew close to the theatre of Teodor Mazilu. A playwright of genius, the author of *Fools in the Moonlight*, has established a literature for the theatre that is rich in special nuances of black humour. Teodor Mazilu is an author of consummate uniqueness, a uniqueness earned through hard work. His plays have gradations, symmetries, powers that relate to visceral psychologies. But the whole is garbed in a precious language, appropriate to a character unique in Romanian literature. Directing a performance of *The Sleepy Adventure* at the National Theatre in Timişoara and *These Hypocritical Fools* at the Hungarian State Theatre in Cluj, I discovered a filiation between Shakespeare's fools and Teodor Mazilu's fools. In Mazilu, the fools are sick and pain the soul because of their human deformity. Coining for my own use the expression "hypocritical clowns," I have tried to define this concept.

A quotation from Fyodor Sologub's *The Petty Demon* will serve me as a motto for the attempt to mediate on Mazilu's characters:

If your gaze lingers a little too long on his quick, precise movements, you might think that he is not a living man, that he does not live, or that he has never lived, that he sees nothing that takes place in the living world, hears nothing but the sounds of words bereft of meaning.

In Mazilu's theatre, old judges of injustice and lies fall ill and their vocation deteriorates. We can never forget Shakespeare's fools. When silence was under lock and key, they opened up the truths pent in darkness and uttered them, braving and judging moral evil. In Mazilu, on the other hand, the fools become great villains. Mazilu closely observes stupidity with the precision of a Geiger counter. His clowns are dangerous. Mazilu's comedy arises in concordance with Nietzsche's theorem: "Comedy as a release of nausea at the absurd."

I remember a line spoken by a fool in Shakespeare's *Twelfth Night*: "Foolery, sir, does walk about the orb like the sun, it shines everywhere." In Mazilu's plays we will find the symptoms of classic and modern folly. Influenced by the theatre of the absurd, Mazilu creates a special humour. Recently, a prestigious critic wrote an essay about Mazilu's theatre in which he names the late playwright "a Gogol who has read Camus." Mazilu's fools frighten you. This is because the fools have fallen sick.

Whenever something essential is decided, somebody always comes and asks a question. Constantin Zărnescu, a writer from Cluj, has a question to put.

His puzzlement and alarm concern a myth that has come down through the centuries. His play, titled *Queen Jocasta*, sensitises our thought to an archetype named after and embodied by Oedipus. Through a successful and courageous artistic act, Constantin Zărnescu astonishes our souls, awakening them from slumber along with the great myth of Sophocles's *Oedipus Rex*.

We must acknowledge that the Romanian writer brings into discussion the very basis of Sophocles's dramatic construct. Here, I cannot but recall a cultural act of similar courage, that of Gabriel Liiceanu, who, in a book about the *concept of tragedy*, rejects the Aristotelean theory of the tragic. Both attitudes are provocative.

Constantin Zărnescu brings the tragedy of Oedipus up to date, but he does so from a different viewpoint than Sophocles's. The viewpoint is paradoxical. Let me quote from the Prologue: "Sophocles showed us only what a man could do in cruel, tragic history; the other side of the coin now remains to be seen, i.e. what a woman could have done if she had had political rights both in life and on the stage, if she had ever emerged from the *gynaeceum* to reveal her life, her suffering, her misfortunes."

The question is indeed paradoxical. We would never have thought of such an ideatic position. Zărnescu reinvents the myth and brings it to light for us in a way that is astonishing. It is a fascinating demonstration. I was enthralled by this shift in the emphasis of the tragedy. After I finished the book, I remembered a real event I once read about: Bertrand Russell's famous letter to Gottlob Frege, which he sent just as the latter was completing his magnum opus. Laying out his famous paradox, the young Russell undermined Frege's whole life's work.

Similarly, I experience *Queen Jocasta* as an undermining of the myth. Why not be honest? Hitherto, nobody has thought of inverting the emphasis. Nobody has thought about the problem of Jocasta. Nobody has developed the psychology of Jocasta. For, the Queen Mother is an archetypal figure, too. As French anthropologist Gilbert Durand said, "The Great Mother is without doubt the most universal religious and psychological entity" (*Anthropological Structures of the Imaginary*). Zărnescu sets out from the existing symbolic stage properties, but he reinterprets them.

Throughout the dramatic construct there is a modern acerbity. The myth is interiorised and experienced in a fantastical mode. There is toil, a search for the absolute, obloquy, a curse that bars the writer's way in his empathetic enterprise. Made to protect her very being, Jocasta conceals the secret, she tries to prevent the catastrophe, but in the end, she is sacrificed without mercy. King Oedipus bears a heavy burden of responsibility toward Queen Jocasta, his mother. He who picks at what time has scabbed over makes a terrifying mistake. Oedipus is guilty.

The writer makes a strange reference: the *theme of noon*. Oedipus kills at noonday, inflamed by the heat of the sun, blinded by the light and the dust.

The act is described in such a way as to seem gratuitous. The overwhelming suggestion is that the act of Oedipus and that of Meursault in *The Stranger* are identical.

Hurrying through town, I often see a sight that moves me: people sitting on benches in parks reading, summer, spring, autumn. I consider the act of reading within view of other people particularly beautiful thanks to its honesty. Absorbed in their books, women and men, young and old, they gradually distance themselves from the world, life, nature, other people. To read in the sight of strangers means to accept a role, willy-nilly. In the films of Jean-Luc Godard I am struck deeply by the fact that his favourite books appear. A character will be carrying a book and sometimes he will even read from it aloud. To open a book in front of others is something sacred and beautiful since it presupposes trust among people.

In my production of Goethe's *Iphigenia in Tauris* in Petroşani, the female protagonist opens a book in a difficult, grief-stricken moment. The tears dry on her cheeks and a secret monologue, conveyed through her reading of the book, becomes her guide through the night. To seek the help of a book means to acknowledge that the light of the word vanquishes the darkness of solitude.

In regard to difficult moments and the need to seek the help of a particular book, I must confess that often I like to reread Lucian Raicu's essay *Gogol, or the Fantasticality of the Banal*. It is a brilliant exegesis. The book has a rare musicality. In it, Gogol's greatness, his labours, his aura, his fear of women, his loneliness, his illness, his genius are blazing entities. The author transcends the function of critic and composes a poem about a fate so strange and so singular. Every time I read it, it harrows me, making me think not only of the power of fate, but also the artistic fruits of a life, Gogol's, that sings its own end. Lucian Raicu's essay tells us that art is not only a celebration, but also entails a huge sacrifice on the part of its creator, for the sake of other people and immortality.

The other day, I reread my musings on my production in Petroşani. In the programme I published my thoughts on the text and the production. These thoughts are all that remain now that the production is over. Rereading them is greatly moving.

1   Above all else, this sacred text focuses an obsession. Its soaring words are Goethe's encounter with a sublime, essential archetype: the Eternal Feminine.

2 The Feminine is the strangest alloy of gold and light, the deepest well-spring of immortality and blessed frenzy, the most beautiful sound-wave of all the galaxies' music. Woman is the final deity that our old Earth brings forth, since she is the child and mysterious, holy bride of Wisdom.

3 Goethe is beloved because his attitudes are utopian, idealist, but also sidesplittingly funny.

4 The litmus test will be a fanatical performance by young actors. Goethe will be decked with the heavy, blazing, emperor's cloak of the twentieth century.

5 Reading *Iphigenia in Tauris*, I think of the *Diary of Anne Frank*; I am reminded of Buchenwald, of Auschwitz. The mystery of Kafka stalks us here; like the blazing image of "In the Penal Colony," we curse the anti-human system that is fascism.

6 At this performance of the play on a beautiful spring night, I realise that old Goethe becomes the contemporary of the sly Samuel Beckett.

7 Might Goethe have been waiting for Godot too?

8 Mirela Cioabă, in the role of Iphigenia, is a dazzling spirit in whom even the shadows become blinding. In her the flame is alive. In word and gesture, she creates poetic explosions of actorly release. Through her power, the Feminine earns the right to eternity.

9 We aim for a performance in which two great theorists of the theatre will come together: Artaud and Brecht. The actor creates savage emphases within a system that is ironic, critical, distanced from swirling emotion. The actor is released. The system of acting is lucid, but incendiary.

10 Our performance is experimental. The elements of the theatrical code comprise a ceremony whereby we cast a glance at the age of Goethe, but behind us we have the moral axis of the century to come. A bridge is flung across an abyss. Iphigenia guides us and teaches us the mysterious love of our fellow man.

A director must love the characters of the dramatic text. Here he is at the table, reading. The actors have gathered around him. Some smile, some frown, they are tense. Most of them feign indifference, although their souls quiver with pleasure. For nothing is more celebratory than the first reading, around the table. From that very first moment a pure and loving relationship is created. If he loves the characters, the director will love the actors. It is always well that there be an actress in the main role. The purity of the relationship between the director and the first lady might be said to possess something of the consuming, fantastic power of conquering the spiritual heights. The Eternal Feminine keeps watch over the path through the labyrinth. The model is Beatrice summoning Dante. The road is hard, exhausting, but the beauty of ennobled creation will warm the crystals of ice and spring will envelop the stage.

Reviewing my programme notes for the premiere of Barbu Ştefănescu-Delavrancea's *The Second Conscience* at the National Theatre in Cluj, I feel a slight unease. Seeking the truth of the text, did I really bring its semantic richness to light?

Let me reread it:

1   A story constructed from events such as those in *The Second Conscience* can only take place in a space sacralised by symbols and starkness. I say this in order to prepare the viewer, who I wish to be lucid and to remain at our side in our attempt at purification through leaving the everyday behind and setting off in search of the mirror's depths.

2   The author proves to be a genuine visionary. And at the same time, he is a subtle commentator of a particular social ill. The story of Rudolf, which is girded in the armour of poetry, diagnoses the malady to which we today apply a scientific term: dual personality.

3   We can conceive of man only as a whole man. Heightened differences between the *person* (the social mask) and the *ego* (the need for intimacy) represent a dangerous alienation. In such cases, as Herbert Marcuse says, the reason is no longer in agreement with pleasure. A dual personality is a kind of deviltry.

4   I read this text with passion and a genuine desire for purification. It is strange how a protagonist who possesses social standing collapses once he becomes conscious that he conceals a vice.

5   I wonder what kind of passion one might feel toward the *Mona Lisa*. I wonder what kind of man Rudolf is. He is fated to meet a woman like the Gioconda, a physical embodiment of that painting. Melanie is a fury, a demigod who arrives from afar to punish a fanatical man, a pleasure-seeking, evil man. Boundlessly in love with a face that for him erases the outlines of the world and all its troubles, Rudolf displays a weakness that will be fatal to him. In contact with the abyss, making tangible an inner evil, exposing what is hidden to the light, the protagonist takes the decision to cast himself into death. It is hence that the finale of our performance derives. That which is edifying in a man's life can only be the desire for purity and the purification of a whole man grimly determined to mark out the boundaries of virtue. As Kant said, the beautiful is man's starry firmament and moral soul.

6   We intend a performance verging on the fantastical, with hints of ancient tragedy, and at the same time we attempt to distance ourselves from the text slightly, so that the actor will be a step ahead of the character and

therefore able to comment on him, avoiding contamination by mental illness as a result of so-called identification with the character.

The previous text was titled *The Need for Purity* and took its motto from Heidegger: "Being is permeated by veiled fatality, situated between the divine and the anti-divine." The words cannot but bring back to me the ascetic cruelty of a very stark performance.

Sometimes, even if you oppose it with all your being, a ritual is stillborn. The actors sense it from the very beginning. The road is wrong. But something stronger than we are leads us down that road. The imponderability of the theatre is stifled and a clumsy mechanism sends us hurtling along the rails over the precipice. The plummet is all the more terrifying when it is foreseen. I have experienced such an absurd event a number of times. It hasn't happened often. The road taken by such an attempt is uninteresting. We try to do our duty. We go by the letter of the text, but we blame the author, then the set designer, then the director, and finally the actors, and even the audience. Awful. Something unseen has seeped into this vain endeavour and the theatrical act is no more able to rid itself of it than the body can its shadow while standing in the sun. This phenomenon dogged me mostly in my early years in theatre, but it was more ferocious later. In Jassy, in Timişoara, and in Timişoara again a few years ago, with a play by the late Teodor Mazilu.

I am so intimidated by Chekhov that had I not been invited by the Reşiţa Theatre to put on *The Seagull* I would never have dared make the attempt. I experience a strange feeling on rereading the programme notes. I realise the attempt was successful. Should I or should I not be satisfied? The thoughts expressed in the notes, titled "The Comedy of Privacy, or The Behind-the-Scenes of the Gods," remain the same:

1 The new criticism, whose constellation of famous names includes Roland Barthes, who is closest to what I feel, has abandoned all interest in the writer as a person.
2 Our turbulent century has killed, among other things, the importance of a writer's biography.
3 The artwork dwells alone, in the light, gleaming like a divine diamond, cruelly forgetful of him who gave it life. Is this a good thing? I think so.
4 Never has a biography added less to the huge meaning of an artwork. I am thinking of Beethoven, Mozart, Stravinsky, Michelangelo, De Chirico, Dostoyevsky, Gogol, and others. The life of an artist is like a handful of dust. . . . The light belongs not to him, but to his song.

5   I have known many artists, but I have not tried to encroach on their privacy precisely because I wished to go on deifying them.

6   The theme of *The Seagull* is the wretched, wounded privacy of four artists: Treplev, Nina, Arkadina, and Trigorin. Around them can be found mediocre characters, who accompany them on their tortured journey.

7   We do not know whether they are great artists. It matters little. Chekhov describes not an artwork, but a biography. And he describes it in order to make us understand that art is not possible without suffering. To make us sympathise with the artist, the creator.

8   Anthropologist Gilbert Durand says of a certain kind of creator: "A threepenny person creates a work worth a hundred thousand francs." The modest, quiet, timid Johann Sebastian Bach falls within this category.

9   It might seem that Chekhov advises nobody to encroach on the privacy of an artist. I sadly think of the tortured, senseless solitude of Kafka. I seek to understand why Gorki wrote to Chekhov: "Anton Pavlovich, you are colder than the devil." The truth is that Chekhov has no pity for his characters. It is like when you see a shot bird plummet to the ground; at bottom, Chekhov's play is ferocious. On the surface, in appearance, this world displays a certain elegance. But it is the elegance of a leper dressed for a soirée. It is this disguise that interests us.

10   In our performance there will be two spaces. One will convey the banality and misery of an uninteresting life. This will be the main stage. For the second space, the scenographer will construct a magic box with mirrors and traditional Russian dolls. This will be the sacral space, the ivory tower, the stage within a stage.

11   Unflinchingly, with the cruelty specific to Chekhov, our performance will map out the destiny of the artist, and it will become an essay on life and art.

12   We wish our journey to be hopeful. We are to understand that above all else Chekhov demanded of the artist that he love people and secondly that he sacrifice himself for them.

13   In regard to Chekhov's characters, I think of Gogol's fear of cold once his great talent had been exhausted.

14   I don't really know what kind of writer Treplev is, but his surly, discontented character, his pride, his pose of being an outcast make me dislike him. He carries his cross, almost ready to be absolved through meaningless toil, when all of a sudden, a terrible fact about him is revealed to us: his soul is a desert. A Fata Morgana has led him away from the wellspring and into the endless night. By his suicide he fulfils a pact with the devil. Not one glimmer of human hope has lit his destiny. Of him one might say, quoting Kierkegaard: "The flowers of my soul are flowers of ice."

15   Not one of the four artists in *The Seagull* knows how to delight in art. Their art is joyless. A terrifying sterility carries them down the road

of emptiness and suffering. Elevated brilliance turns its back on them, their horizon darkens, and groping in the dark, mediocre, they will be incapable of warming our hearts in any way. The coldness emanated by their dead art will terrify us.

16 Like their art, their private lives are nothing but a banal collection of meaningless events. *The Seagull* can be read in parallel with Camus's *The Myth of Sisyphus*. These artists will not be redeemed through their work, not even in an absurd, existential sense.

17 The death of Nina's child darkens the emotive structure and brings with it the coldness of the ending, amplifying Nina's lostness in this mediocre world.

I don't know whether the foregoing notes, prompted by a performance, have any value in themselves. I think not. And in general, almost everything that is written is of no great value in relation to Theatre. The Theatrical Art is a phenomenon so alive that it cannot be contained in written words. You cannot convey the magical effect of theatre's complex, vital movements. In a way, those of us who toil at writing do so in vain. I find release in writing, but only in order to prepare myself to accept an invitation to *do theatre*. Without it I don't think I could carry on living.

D. R. Popescu once told me that in order to stage Aeschylus your hair first had to turn white. He was right. A young soul cannot lament seriously. The vitality necessary to wisdom is only overwhelmed by the tragic in life's final moments. I think you need to have a consciousness of death, to feel its presence around you, as Tolstoy said, if you are to succeed in conveying symbols as blinding as the sun. I would like to stage a text by Aeschylus one day. I would create a production that drew on the mysteries of the pyramid of Cheops, which at the same time would be as vital as ancient Indian painting. How I regret that D. R. Popescu never got to see my production of Seneca's *Medea*.

I put on Seneca's *Medea* in Turda. I would define the performance as a study, as theatrical research. We sought modern tools to construct a tragicomic phenomenon. I don't believe in performances where the comic or the tragic each unfold absolutely separately. Shakespeare's demonstration of combining the comic and the tragic has been dominant through time. We put on a polemical production at Café la Mama in New York, in which, with the young and talented Turda State Theatre company, we attempted to construct a *buffonata* shot through with terror. As we worked, we were thinking of Fellini's *Satyricon*.

The dramatic text defines the kind of society with which its author was contemporary; Seneca was the victim of a Caligula-type society. Today, this type of society provides food for thought. Our century has been confronted with such societies, fascism remains vivid in our memories, and we are alarmed by sporadic outbreaks of neo-Nazism. The production took a critical look at a society dominated by blood and murder. In the form of theatrical research, the production applied commedia dell'arte procedures to a dramatic structure to which other ancient ceremonial procedures might equally apply. I chose commedia dell'arte techniques in order to lend the performance a comic, *buffo* look, beneath the mask of which would be sensed seams of bloody tragedy.

The performance was constructed through improvisation. I have long dreamed of theatre that would come into being the same as jazz does in New Orleans. I also think that there are similarities between commedia dell'arte and jazz. The scenographic idea of dressing the characters in costumes borrowed from Kabuki and Nō theatre emphasised the ritual aspect, lending it a vigorously aesthetic ancestral weight. It is a pity that it was performed only once.

I once rehearsed a performance with Irina Petrescu. The play was never staged, but the memory of Irina Petrescu has remained in my soul, a secret treasure. To me, Irina Petrescu's talent is without compare. To do theatre with Irina Petrescu is to celebrate every minute. Her smile, her fathomless gaze, the rare beauty of her being, her acting, her playfulness, the dance of her words and her body, her respiration, her battle against the stereotypical all come together to form the petals of a "subterranean flower," as Novalis would say, a flower which, springing up in the light of the theatre, tames and heals spite and emptiness.

So beautifully does Irina Petrescu act that a director's emotions are purified in her presence. The crust of indifference and endless boredom is stripped away and, his attention aroused by her pure, radiant lucidity, he becomes witness to a gaze that penetrates the mysteries. It pains me to think that so many directors either overlook Irina Petrescu without understanding her or understand too little of that regal flame that ought to be allowed to burn, overflowing with the strange sentiments of a unique talent.

At the end of Peter Brook's production of *A Midsummer Night's Dream*, the actors of the Royal Shakespeare Company came down from the stage and shook hands with the audience. The actress playing Titania stood before me, held out her hand. I gripped that beautiful, warm hand and to this day (fifteen years have elapsed since then) I cannot forget that moment, which was one of the most beautiful in my life. To shake hands with an actress from London in a theatre in Bucharest was something unique and amazing. All the barriers of the world came toppling down, the theatre burned down the wall of isolation, proving yet again that art unites people through profound meditation on life, love, death, sacred moments of our passage through this world.

Constantin Cubleşan, from Cluj, has written a wonderful play, a theatrical text full of depth and meaning: *Flight From the Nest*. It moved me and with all my soul I wished to put on a performance of the play, in which all the harrowing problems of the protagonists would acquire the powerful expression of an archetype. With my friend and collaborator, scenographer T. Th. Ciupe, I conceived a striking format for the production. I must confess that seldom have I met a set designer so deep and so talented, so imaginative and so sensitive as T. Th. Ciupe, despite his striking modesty.

Constantin Cubleşan is a reserved man, but a bold writer. Behind the words of his play lie hidden a disquiet that burns dogmas with a branding iron. I wanted our production to be bathed in a light like that of dawn, when the darkness flees in terror from the glorious sun, ruler of the clear sky. I thought about how we always need the silence in which we can be sure of our actions.

In Constantin Cubleşan's play we encounter an architect. Above all else, to be human means to build a home where we can shelter from the storm, from the darkness. I wanted to convey to the audience a mood that was both pleasant and unpleasant, quiet and unquiet, like fire, which warms, but also burns. By authenticity in this world and in this life, I understand sacrifice. In this life, whoever wishes to take pleasure only in the senses merely swells the number of the indifferent and cynical. Only one way of life is worthy: to bear witness to the love of one's fellow man through sacrifice.

The future remembers only those who have given mankind the toil of sleepless nights. It is of such a hero that Constantin Cubleşan speaks. But as the architect of the play, the author brings to the fore a paradoxical situation by means of the troubling presence of two women. I do not like to utter their names. With the actresses who played them, I named them the Black Swan and the White Swan, archetypes dear to Tchaikovsky. The importance of these two characters is overwhelming, since it is before Woman that the creator responds to Destiny the most profoundly. Based on the clash between virtue and error, the performance acquired a solemn garb, supporting the unconfessed words and the silences of a simple and mysterious emotion.

What can be said of an actor? Having given himself body and soul to so many characters, what remains of him for himself? Nothing? On the contrary. An actor is so inwardly rich that there is never enough time to get to know him. I speak of those actors who have a fanatical faith in the theatre, lit radiantly by their talent. In fact, one should not even try to get to know an actor, the same as any other artist. An artist, and here I think of actors too, is so caught up in his art that it would be blasphemous to encroach on his privacy, where curiosity has no purpose. In any event, I don't really want to get to know actors off-stage. I cannot help but agree with the French poet who said, "Living? Our servants will do that for us."

When I met Vali Zitta I experienced a powerful emotion. Behind her playful gaze lay hidden a mood of fathomless sadness. It was as if I were trying to divine a mystery. I found before me a complex being. I came to know her talent and I realised that Vali Zitta could create that diaphanous mixture of the real and supra-real that tints certain magical moments of our lives. Zitta was able to embody an appearance which you, as a spectator, scratched at anxiously, wounding the character in order to discover her secret, her mystery.

But above all else, Zitta can act. And she does so with matchless exaltation. In Tudor Mușatescu's *Titanic Waltz* and Teodor Mazilu's *These Hypocritical Fools*, both of which I staged at the Hungarian State Theatre in Cluj, she confirmed her frenetic wit, her inventiveness, her wonderful acting. You cannot help but be infected with the pleasure and joy of it.

Vali Zitta knows the mystery of the novel gesture. Her resources of eurhythmy, ballet, and clownish play, as well as the cry, the whisper, the song, are inexhaustible. When I first met Zitta, I immediately pictured her in a tragedy such as Euripides's *Elektra*. Zitta is a cautious artist. Her feminine caution guards her against the ridiculous. But once a director has won her trust (see *The Night Shelter*, directed by Harag), she becomes an Ariel serving the idea of art's power for the good, swooping through the firmament.

My first production for the puppet theatre was a production of *Cinderella*, dramatised by Al. Căprariu. Although it was my first attempt at the medium, I wanted it to be an experimental production. The context was auspicious and my attempt was a success. My intention, as I recall it now, was to construct a series of shows with the management and talented actors of the Puppet Theatre. My artistic struggle was aimed at attaining a higher convention. I wanted to define myself as a director by taking the side of now illusion, now reality. Reading Edmund Burke's *Philosophical Enquiry Into the Origin of Our Ideas of the Sublime and Beautiful*, I was struck in particular by the idea he develops in the following paragraph:

> The first and the simplest emotion which we discover in the human mind is Curiosity. By curiosity, I mean whatever desire we have for, or whatever pleasure we take in novelty. We see children perpetually

running from place to place to hunt out something new; they catch with great eagerness and with very little choice, at whatever comes before them; their attention is engaged by every thing, because every thing has, in that stage of life, the charm of novelty to recommend it.

I used the quotation as the motto in a theoretical exposition that sought to persuade the puppeteers of the seriousness of the experiment I wished to engage in. Opinions were divided, but the experiment succeeded, and at a recent arts festival for children I won a director's prize. Today, convinced in my innermost self that it is the sincerity of those who create a production that makes it viable, I remember my intentions at the beginning of a path that has continued and will continue in the service of art for children. Therefore, let me reproduce a theoretical argument in which I wholeheartedly believe:

We are interested above all in the psychological reality of the child. The direction taken by the production of Al. Căprariu's play about Cinderella was guided by a real event arising from an attitude on the part of my small daughter. I had tried a number of times to tell her stories using puppets. Hidden behind a screen, I did what puppeteers usually do. I was astounded when, ten minutes after I had started working the puppets, altering my voice, my daughter came behind the screen to watch my efforts in amusement. Instead of letting herself be deceived by the illusion, she watched with intelligent interest the mechanism of handling the puppets. I was faced with a curiosity that ironised my attempts to create an illusion. This event within the family constituted the psychological source of the production I was to put on. I think it is sometimes necessary to confront children with the truth. More often than not children astound us by the sheer intelligence of their questions. Why should we not have faith in stripping away illusion as a path to a higher convention? This century of ours, with all its upheavals and its startling social achievements, belongs not only to adults but also to children. I believe that we should not underestimate the intuitive abilities of the most beautiful and the most honest age of life. One only has to go to an exhibition of children's art to be astonished by the strange depths and the higher artistic conventions. It is due to a higher attitude toward the child that we wish to create a performance that is as truthful as it is beautiful. We have adopted Huizinga's idea that play preceded culture. Huizinga argues that neither puppies nor children need to wait for culture in order to play. Hence the conclusion that *play* is a strange, an ineffable phenomenon.

I believe first of all in the joy and power of the child to take part in *play*. When we watch the educative process in kindergartens, we remember and we observe the extraordinary enthusiasm of the child when placed within a ludic situation. Masks, costumes, sets, plays awaken in the child strong impulses toward the ineffable essence of *play*. I do not wish to deny either the pleasure children take in a *magic show*, in which the puppets are worked by forces unknown to the child. Our society today is rational above all else. I even wonder how long today's child will accept the illusion of the puppet theatre without asking questions. It is our duty to regard audiences of children as higher audiences. The world's great directors have regarded the child as the most sensitive critic of a theatrical performance. Whoever has read Stanislavski's *My Life in Art* will remember that he was assured of the success of a performance if it was attractive to a child. Preserving a sense of proportion, I too can say that my diploma production of Ibsen's *Rosmersholm*, staged in Sibiu, was watched with particular interest by a number of children in rehearsal. My observations consolidate an apologia for the contemporary child. Along with the arithmetic and theory of crowds, today's child has entered the domain of symbolic functions. And it is our duty that we keep pace with current events. In fact, what we want above all is a performance in which children will be drawn into a game. The actors who are cast, no more than three, will animate the puppets in full view. Obviously, within this convention, the actor will be an integral element of the artistic format. The aesthetic of the game must become striking. With the theatre's set designer, I have conceived appropriate costumes for them. It is exactly as if the actors too were part of the fairy tale being narrated. Apprentice sorcerers and officiants, they represent the limitless human power to animate matter. By ritual means, we aim to enchant the children. And since adults actually conceal inner children, we aim for a performance that will be attractive to all ages. The action will take place in a puppet workshop. As the author says, addressing the children in the audience: "Children, my story is about a little girl who was left an orphan." The officiants will address lines to the children, sharing the roles among themselves. Through this vision we will find ourselves at the spatial centre of the sorcerers who are the people who animate inert matter. Let it be understood that there will be a *principal animator* of puppets, who will create the convention with the audience. She will deliver the lines of the clown, as well as taking on other roles. The secondary animators will create what Peter Brook achieved with his extras in the Royal Shakespeare Company production of *A Midsummer Night's Dream*: the extras who, watching with pleasure, sadness, joy, enthusiasm, irritation what was happening on stage, created through their attitudes a psychic halo around the protagonists. The Central Animator's assistants will be a kind of mirror audience for the children.

The children will be drawn into the game. Beneath their intelligent eyes the sets will spring into view, the spotlights will shine, and through the technique of puppet theatre the performance will reproduce the power of the human will. At the same time, the performance will be an essay on the puppet theatre itself. The battle between what is good and evil in the soul will parallel the battle between appearance and essence. We will win the children over to our theatre, they will join in the games initiated by the Animator. It will be aimed primarily at children and secondarily at adults. Through our performance the child will discover that the true creator of material and spiritual values is *man*. In conclusion, let me recall the reaction of my young daughter when I was struggling to animate puppets hidden behind a screen and let me say that through that reaction, through her curiosity and irony, she revealed to me something essential: the majority of children demonstrate a *critical awareness*.

This theoretical argument was my guide during my work at the Puppet Theatre in Cluj. The crowning achievement of this argument proved to be a major production based on Mozart's *Magic Flute*, a ritualistic performance with the actors on view. But gradually, the puppet in itself has gained a deeper importance in my eyes and today I am interested in overcoming difficulties and problems related to the magical essence of the true Puppet Theatre.

The theatre becomes a sacred art through the living presence of the unmasked, unmediated protagonist. It is the art in which man witnesses at first hand the glorification or sacrificing of the protagonist. This is why it is meet that we speak of the theatre in solemn, sacerdotal terms. Sometimes I am terrified when I think of the fragility of a performance. After a few performances, a production becomes alienated in its structure. As it has no fixed parameters, the lability of this art makes me shudder. Nevertheless, we always witness the resurrection of the protagonist without remembering the perishability that defines him. In my innermost self, I crave theoretical foundations for my art. Each of us imagines the history of the theatre in his own way. We are obliged to have a little story, something like a prayer, which we recite in our moments of solitude in order to assuage our sufferings, in the belief that this art and Thalia, its terrible, tutelary muse, are immortal. The little story I have made for myself is called *The True Path*. I transcribe it here as a statement of faith:

The theatre was born from the fear of solitude. In origin the theatrical performance was religious. The forces of nature, too violent for frail humankind, were tamed by those who acted out the mystical drama. In time, theatre became secular. But never has theatre denied its collective nature. For a time, actors were condemned by the Church. Today, the myth of the actor is at its pinnacle. Today's society, in its need for culture, has created theatrical temples. Buildings traditional and modern vie in architectural splendour and theatrical technology to attract audiences. There is a so-called theatrological convention. By purchasing a ticket, the spectator has the right to enjoy a theatrical performance. There is a freely accepted regulation whereby, if the spectator does not like the performance, it cannot be halted while in progress. People are eager for artistically successful performances. There is today a fashion in the theatre. A strange creator has arisen in the history of the theatre: the *director*. With him arose the original interpretation of the dramatic text. The audience is given an individual vision of the drama. The style of the performance is created by the meeting of dramatic text, director, scenographer and actors. Many philosophers have been sceptical as to whether the theatrical art would last. Nevertheless, in centuries past and in the twentieth century in particular, the theatrical performance has enjoyed huge success. We will talk first of all about the actor. The actor is a being who lends an image to the dramatic character. The actor as a person is not interesting. Although the tabloids in the West publish sensational stories about actors' lives, we believe the actor is a person like any other. The artistic process of embodying a character on stage is a phenomenon that arises from so-called acting technique.

Although the Theatre Institute tries to reduce the act of embodying a character on stage to a common denominator, we believe and constantly observe that every actor possesses his or her own personal technique. The actor's working method depends on his or her psychosomatic make-up. The actor's constitution, his or her emotive system, his or her ability to rationalise concrete facts, his or her imagination, all these come together to create a unique mimetic process. Over the course of time, the process of imitating psychological reality has been enriched through frenzied theatrical imagination, culminating in the present. I believe above all in an art that symbolises truth. Directors such as Meyerhold, Vakhtangov, Tairov, followed by others such as Eugenio Barba, Grotowski and Peter Brook have consolidated an imaginative-symbolic manner of acting. The character is an enigma decipherable at the close of a performance. The supreme judgement breaks down the artistic performance into symbols. The actor becomes an original creator. Only the future will tell how long this form of imagination, this current mode of creation will endure. The actor remains a creator of unique forms. Even if he imitates reality, even if in his creation he is intuitive, rather than an adept of reason, we see only two possibilities in the future of his art. He will be an adept of either verisimilitude or of allegory. But whichever the case, we will rejoice in his psychological successes. It is possible to speak of the director only in the same terms. The quarrel between Stanislavski and Meyerhold has lost none of its currency. This revolt against the real or the acceptance of the real is a dilemma with a history behind it. Whether theatre is poetic, constructing metaphor, or whether it is strictly realistic, it is the audience that will make the value judgement. But the whole of theatrological technique can only be inert matter in comparison with the spirituality of the drama.

The most important theatrical creator remains the author of the dialogue. Without the playwright, the whole light organ of stage effects remains a lifeless object. All the tools of the stage will serve the Word. The immense light brought by the word, the entry via the word into the labyrinth lit by speech, proves to be a portal to essence. In esoteric writings, the ceremony may or not be present, but the unravelling of *enigma-words* is the greatest possible joy. In the theatre, I think we should adopt the opinion of Dutch philosopher Huizinga that performance is a sacral celebration. The emergence from the ordinary, the celebration of culture and of a Sunday well spent, is the satisfaction of him who applauds all the elements of theatre: the spectator. I think that we should sometimes bring the spectator and the director face to face. Through dialogue the director will understand that the real path to him who rejoices in the success of the performance and is saddened when it fails will be the path to the highest emotion. The director is obliged to adopt an attitude of dignity. Spiritual elevation in the secular sense of the word will be the law of the theatre. No dignity is possible outside the word or the spoken word. Nothing seems to me more trivial than the grey and desolate flight from the truth. In symbolic forms or real images, the performance speaks through the word. Outside the word there is no theatre. We do not wish to disregard the power of the mise-en-scène, but we regard it as a secondary creativity, a secondary language. The performance, like every other artistic product, *is enclosed and rests within itself*, as Heidegger says. Broken down into its elements, structuralised, the performance brings unfathomable depths when there is a dual allegory of both words and staging. The pleasure of taking part in the game comes from solving the enigma. In its depths, the performance encloses moral philosophy. But it happens only seldom that theatre constructs a so-called model to be emulated. In its dialectic, more than affirmation of what is good in the soul, the performance is a negation of what is bad in the character. In the theatre there is no exemplary history of protagonists. Seldom does the lawgiver appear. On the other hand, lawlessness stalks the stage. Every playwright will be docilely followed by the theatre company when his protagonists are lawgivers whom we are inclined to follow. The supreme human judgement, at the end of the performance, will choose between what is good and what is bad. I believe in the exceptional power of dramaturgy. Through dialogue the redemptive true enters the stage. In the beginning of the theatre was the Word. The history of the theatre is a history of the drama. The lance cast by Aeschylus flies down the centuries, crossing the spirit of the theatre.

In our native land, Caragiale, followed today by writers such as D. R. Popescu, Marin Sorescu and the late Teodor Mazilu, show us the true path. By following them, we will draw to our side the words spoken and unspoken whose flames and whose play warm our hearts. Life is born through speech. The director will hide in the shadow of the actor called upon to inspire fear or joy.

For a long time, I have been thinking of a performance of a play by Aeschylus. I am fascinated by the *Agamemnon* in particular, an insinuating "mythology of misfortune." Aeschylus's protagonists seek to discover the outcomes of their actions, attempting to divine the future. But the world around us is full of incomprehensible mysteries. The gods become tutelary figures whose will is followed relentlessly. Overwhelmed by the play of fate, humans find themselves at the heart of a dark religion. Deprived of freedom of thought, when they act they are haunted by fears, believing that what the god brings transcends all human possibility. Humans become the plaything of Fate, but Fate is unfathomable. At the beginning of the play, the Messenger says:

> I shall take advantage of the dice that have fallen well for my masters—
> this beacon-watch has thrown me a triple six!
>
> (Trans. Alan H. Sommerstein)

This is a world of roulette players. The stake for which the gods play is man. Never has a play been more heart-rending in its portrayal of a life lived according to chance. According to this concept, chance rules fate and you can have no certainty or faith in what you have to win or lose. Fate is fickle, and the man elevated today will be cast down tomorrow. All the wealth of a man who sets out on a long voyage is shattered by a hidden rock. But equally, today's vanquished will be tomorrow's victor. How can one live according to such an interpretation of life? There seems to be only one answer: to be just and to do nothing to excess. This existential dictum dominates the morals of the time. Under threat of divine retribution, men must avoid committing moral outrages. Nevertheless, experience says that no life can be unblemished. For, "Only the gods live immortal and without pain." Therefore, man, subject to the dictatorship of the gods, can expect cruel defeats, which arrive from the dark unknown. Man carries with him a terrible fate. Helen was born to bring about the fall of Troy. A primal guilt, accompanied by fear, something enigmatic and perilous, permeates the world of the heroes. I think that we may affirm with certainty that the *absurd*, the irrational, is embedded in these primitive events. The anxious personality is defined at the very beginning of world theatre:

> Why, why does this fear
> persistently hover about,
> standing guard in front of my prophetic heart?
> (Trans. Alan H. Sommerstein)

We find ourselves in a domain, in an ancestral space in which fear goes hand in hand with violence. Agamemnon returns home from a bloody war, for whose sake he has sacrificed his daughter Iphigenia. Clytemnestra and her lover Aegisthus plot Agamemnon's death. Murder follows upon murder.

> An old act of outrage is wont
> to give birth to a new young outrage,
> which flourishes amid men's suffering,
> at this time or at that, when there comes
> the proper day for its birth
> and to the deity with whom none can war or fight,
> the unholy arrogance of Ruin, black for the house,
> in the likeness of her parents.
> (Trans. Alan H. Sommerstein)

Ascribing to the gods responsibility for the deed, the villains make murder and vice proliferate. Cassandra, a wonder child, is sacrificed in the name of base revenge. Nonetheless, we naturally wonder who is to blame in such a conceptual context? And the answer must be: *man*. I imagine a performance based on this world of darkness, in agitated pursuit of the cruellest interests. I would like the sets to convey the image of a patch of waste ground, strewn with burnt rags, with army boots and helmets. In the background, the terrifying face of an incomprehensible deity will dominate. It is here that Clytemnestra will appear, officiating the sacrifice demanded by the gods. Her queenly costume will be dazzling. When he returns from the war, Agamemnon's clothes are dirty, ragged. War-weary soldiers will seat themselves on the ground, able to eat in peace at last. I would have their uniforms resemble those worn in the First World War.

In a corner of the patch of waste ground, a military band plays a jazz improvisation from the beginning of the performance to its close, as if chance, improvisation also ruled musical instruments as well as human destiny. Cassandra will appear among the soldiers, in the purity of an immaculate white robe, a virgin serving the divine prophecy. The performance must first of all manifest itself as anti-war. But at the same time, it should contain a vehement protest against all violence against human beings. We might say that the parable of Aeschylus's play is contained in the fable told by the wise chorus:

> Just so a man once
> reared in his home an infant lion,
> fond of the nipple but deprived of its milk,
> in its undeveloped time of life
> tame, well loved by children
> and a delight to the old:
> it was much in his arms
> like a young suckling baby,
> gazing bright-eyed at his hand
> and fawning when hunger pressed it.
> But in time it displayed the character
> inherited from its parents; it returned
> thanks to its nurturers
> by making, with destructive slaughter of sheep,
> a feast unbidden.
> The house was steeped in blood,
> an uncontrollable grief to the household,
> a great calamity with much killing.
> What a god had caused to be reared as an inmate of the house
> was a priest of Ruin.
>
> (Trans. Alan H. Sommerstein)

It seems that the meaning of this parable is one of the consequences of the first reconciliation with injustice. To us denizens of the twentieth century, the story of the lion might provide the impetus for a process of gaining awareness. An awareness of a huge threat, of fire and ash. We have grown accustomed to having patience and taking care, we have reconciled ourselves to a kind of beast that we nurture in our own home. We grow up with the threat of a war, and without any great fear, we play with the idea of it. Aware of a likely war, we ought to determine the future, rather than abandoning it to a throw of the dice. *Probability*—a modern concept, but one with which Aeschylus flirted—will have to be comprehended by human reason, through an act of common will, in order to hold sovereign chance in check. Two thousand years ago, the wise Aeschylus issued a warning against the existence of reckless chance.

21 Conclusion

What might I say at the end of this book about William Shakespeare and the Theatre? I would like to pay homage to the tireless servants of the Theatre. To them belongs the praise. To the actor above all. It is the actor who blazes in our sight, eager to share his or her pain and joy in living speech. The actor remains an eternal seeker of the most brilliant power of speech. The actor brings us from time immemorial the subterranean power of lived language, of the living word. The years will pass and finally it will be seen that the vast architecture of the Theatre rests upon the face and the voice of the eternally treasured actor, incomparable in his or her living power. It is to the actor that the following speech is in fact addressed:

> Thyself and thy belongings
> Are not thine own so proper, as to waste
> Thyself upon thy virtues, them on thee.
> Heaven doth with us, as we with torches do;
> Not light them for themselves; for if our virtues
> Did not go forth of us, 'twere all alike
> As if we had them not.
>
> (*Measure for Measure*, Act One,
> Scene One)

Aureliu Manea, 1945–2014

Aureliu Manea was born in Bucharest on 4 February 1945. He studied to be a theatre director under Radu Penciulescu at the Ion Luca Caragiale Institute in Bucharest, graduating in 1968.

His made his debut as a director with a production of Ibsen's *Rosmersholm* at the Sibiu Theatre, which stunned Romania's theatrical world with the originality of its staging, and the press hailed him as a unique new talent.

Throughout his career, he created a large number of theatre and opera productions, as well as puppet shows, creating a repertoire of both Romanian and foreign plays, some of which had never before been performed in Romania, such as Sophocles's *Philoctetes*. He staged performances at theatres in Timişoara, Turda, Ploieşti, Cluj, Sibiu, Jassy, Piatra Neamţ, and elsewhere.

"His creative acts have given rise to debate, controversy, praise, invective, derisive opposition, serious critical analysis, and ultimately acknowledgement: it has been accepted that this is a powerful artistic figure, an independently minded creator, a man of theatrological science, a profound researcher of the dramatic art" (Valentin Silvestru).

He had the greatest respect for actors and his fellow directors. He loved his audience. He remained a constant innovator. He never created two performances alike. He astonished the public with his gifts in experimental productions such as Arnold Wesker's *Seasons* (at the Matei Millo Theatre, Timişoara), but also with classic productions such as Chekhov's *Three Sisters* (at the State Theatre, Ploieşti).

Aureliu Manea regarded the director as an "engineer of the attention," a "dispenser of speech, silence, movement and stillness," a master craftsman of "the structuration of feeling," a "builder by means of visualisation."

"His performances are inherently polemical; they always express a need for purity and truth; they denounce life's stereotypes; they employ a symbolic, plastic language of complexity; they surpass the plot of the play in their suggestiveness. Manea has a style devoid of theatricality; a penetrating artistic mind; a rigorous, exigent professionalism; he precisely situates the psychological space of the performance; he excels in engaging imagination; he is devoted to the theatre to the point of sacrifice" (Ion Cocora).

"Manea is part of that constellation of modern European directors who invent theatrical structures, establish an optimal artistic convention to convey the message and decide upon a style for every performance. His originality has its root in his unshakeable belief that there is an inexorable, flexible, constantly changing relationship among Theatre, Individual and Time, and it is incumbent upon the performance, as a duty, to reveal it and present it to his contemporaries for their positive meditation" (Valentin Silvestru).

For reasons of ill health, he withdrew from theatrical life in 1991. From 1991 until his death on 13 March 2014, he was a patient at the Neuropsychiatric Recuperation and Rehabilitation Centre in Galda de Jos, Transylvania.

In his final years, he wrote a screenplay inspired by life at Galda de Jos. In 2010, Gheorghe Preda directed a short film based on the screenplay, titled *Prăbușirea* (*The Breakdown*). The film was produced by Viorica Samson Manea in partnership with Scharf Film and was shown at the International Festival of Mediterranean Film, Montpellier, in 2012.

At Galda de Jos, he also created his final production: *The Portuguese Letters of Mariana Alcoforado*. The production was staged at the Metropolis Theatre, Bucharest, in 2012. Once again, he stimulated audiences with the modernity of his vision, with the simplicity of his staging, with the aesthetics and dramatism he managed to create after an absence from the theatre of more than twenty years.

Aureliu Manea will go down in history as one of the Romanian directors who revolutionised and reformulated theatre, alongside Liviu Ciulei, Lucian Pintilie, David Esrig, Andrei Șerban, Gheorghe Harag, Alexandru Tocilescu, Cătălina Buzoianu, and Alexa Visarion.

Encouraged by critic Valentin Silvestru and his friends Ion Cocora and Nicolae Prelipceanu, he wrote articles and essays, and published three major books: *Energiile spectacolului* (*The Energies of Performance*), Editura Dacia, 1983; *Spectacole imaginare și Confesiuni* (*Imaginary Performances and Confessions*), Editura Dacia, 1986; and, toward the end of his life, *Texte regăsite, sfîrșitul lumii va fi un clip* (*Rediscovered Texts, the end of the world will be a videoclip*), Editura Casa Cărții de Știință, 2012.

Teatrul Azi magazine, edited by theatre critic Florica Ichim, published *El, vizionarul: Aureliu Manea* (*He, the Visionary: Aureliu Manea*) in 2000, as part of its *Gallery of Romanian Theatre* series, a volume that brought together the books published by the director, along with a selection of interviews, excerpts from reviews, and a list of his productions.

In 1993, he was awarded the Uniter Prize for his lifetime's achievement, and in 1999, the Ploiești City Hall and Toma Caragiu Theatre Diploma of Excellence for Exceptional Merit in Advancement of the Theatrical Art.

In 1992, Gheorghe Preda made a documentary about Aureliu Manea, titled *The Light Around His Body*, which he filmed in 1991, while Manea was staging Seneca's *Medea* at the Turda Municipal Theatre.

In 2005, Cătălin Ştefănescu made a documentary about Aureliu Manea at Galda de Jos, titled *On Theatre, Love of Man and Wildness*.

In 2007, the Bucharest National Theatre Festival was dedicated to Aureliu Manea.

Also in 2007, Justin Ceuca published a book titled *Aureliu Manea, Essay on a DIRECTOR*.

In token of recognition of his contribution to the advancement of Romanian theatre, in August 2014, the Turda Municipal Theatre was renamed the Aureliu Manea Theatre.

"Aureliu Manea—a cornerstone of Romanian theatre" (Georges Banu).

"An artist-prophet, Manea journeys within revolt. He has not yet exhausted the performances in him. And we miss him" (Alexa Visarion).

"The only director from our country whose art has been transformed into a mythology" (Cătălina Buzoianu).

"Teacher that I am, I tell myself that nonetheless never will I be able to teach anybody that which depends on a gift—the style of Aureliu Manea: a Black Pearl" (Maria Vodă Căpuşan).

"Aureliu Manea was to the Romanian theatre what Coco Chanel was to fashion in her day. Director at the Timişoara National Theatre, in the 1970s Mr Manea did theatre in the manner of Grotowski without his knowing it. The actors who worked with him speak of him as an artist touched by the wing of genius" (Adriana Mocca).

Glossary of Romanian directors, actors, playwrights, and writers

Alistair Ian Blyth

Balotă, Nicolae (1925–2014) Literary critic, historian, and essayist. Balotă taught Literature and Philosophy at Cluj University but was sacked in 1948 after his arrest for possession of banned books. Released from prison in 1949, he remained unemployed until his second arrest in 1956, charged with compiling a list of the human rights abuses committed by the Romanian People's Republic. He was released in 1963, after agreeing to write informer's reports for the Securitate, and worked as a researcher at the George Călinescu Institute of Literary History and Theory until he managed to leave the country in 1979, applying for political asylum in the West. From 1981, he taught Comparative Literature at the François Rabelais University, Tours, France. His works include a study of the literature of the absurd, *Lupta cu absurdul* (*The Struggle with the Absurd*) (1971) and *Caietul albastru* (*The Blue Notebook*) (2007), a diary of the totalitarian period.

Banu, Georges (1943–) Major European theatre critic and theorist, expert on the work of Peter Brook, Professor of Theatre Studies at the University of Louvain, member of the Romanian Academy. Born in Buzău, Romania, Banu studied at the Academy of Theatre and Film, Bucharest. In 1973, he emigrated to France, where he taught Theatre Studies at the Sorbonne. He is honorary chairman of the International Association of Theatre Critics. His works include *Théâtre sortie de secours* (Aubier, 1984), *Peter Brook: de Timon d'Athènes à Hamlet* (Flammarion, 1989), *Avec Brecht* (Actes Sud, 1999), *Les Cités du théâtre d'art: de Stanislavski à Strehler* (Éditions théâtrales, 2000), *Les répétitions: de Stanislavski à aujourd'hui* (Actes Sud, 2005), *Peter Brook, vers un théâtre premier* (Points Essais, 2005), *Shakespeare, le monde est une scène: metaphors et pratiques théâtrales* (Gallimard, 2009), and *Amour et désamour du théâtre* (Actes Sud, 2013). A close friend of Aureliu Manea, he followed all his productions.

Bulandra, Lucia Sturdza (1873–1961)   Actress and first lady of the Romanian theatre. A scion of the Sturdzas, an old princely family from Moldavia, she made her stage debut at the Romanian National Theatre in 1898. Her grandfather had forbidden her to use the family name in the theatre billings, an order which she ignored. In 1914, she and her husband, actor Tony Bulandra (1881–1943), established their own company, founding the Queen Maria Theatre, which for decades fostered Romania's greatest acting talents, of whom Bulandra was fiercely protective. The company was forced to disband after the closure of the Queen Maria Theatre during the war, in 1941, and a dark period of seven years ensued, during which Bulandra suffered poverty, a hiatus in her acting career, and the death from cancer of her beloved husband. In 1947, Bulandra was appointed manager of the newly established Bucharest Municipal Theatre, a position she held until her death at the age of ninety-four. The theatre was renamed after her in 1961.

Bulandra Theatre   The Municipal Theatre was founded by Bucharest City Hall in 1947 and its first general manager was Lucia Sturdza Bulandra (q.v.), after whom the institution was subsequently renamed. From 1963 to 1974, the theatre manager was leading Romanian director Liviu Ciulei (q.v.). Since 2002, the theatre manager has been Alexandru Darie. The Bulandra has two auditoriums at two different locations in Bucharest, one named after great Romanian actor and comedian Toma Caragiu (1925–1977), the other after Liviu Ciulei. The history of the theatre is associated with the names of some of Romania's greatest twentieth-century actors: Toma Caragiu, Octavian Cotescu, Clody Berthola, Gina Patrichi, Ileana Predescu, Victor Rebengiuc, Mariana Mihuț, Irina Petrescu (q.v.), Virgil Ogășanu, Rodica Tapaleagă, and Ion Caramitru. During the 1960s and 1970s, the theatre staged major productions of Ion Luca Caragiale's (q.v.) *Carnival Scenes*, Chekhov's *The Cherry Orchard*, and Gogol's *The Government Inspector*. Even during the 1980s, a period of increasing totalitarian repression and economic shortages, there were important productions of *Tartuffe* and *Hamlet*. Since 1991, the Bulandra has been a member of the Union of the Theatres of Europe.

Buzoianu, Cătălina (1938–2019)   Leading Romanian theatre director. After graduating from the Institute of Theatrical and Cinematographic Arts, Bucharest, in 1969, she was assigned as a director to the Vasile Alecsandri National Theatre, Jassy, and went on to work as a director at the Youth Theatre, Piata Neamț. From 1979 to 1985, she was permanent head director at Teatrul Mic (The Little Theatre), Bucharest, and then permanent director at the Bulandra Theatre (q.v.) until her retirement. One of her best-known productions was *A Wasted Morning* at the Bulandra, a stage adaptation of the novel of the same title by Gabriela Adameşteanu (1942–). She also directed films, including a screen version of the Teatrul Mic production of Paul Zindel's *The Effect of Gamma Rays on Man-in-the-Moon Marigolds* in 1977.

Căprariu, Al. (1929–1988)   Poet and philosopher. He was editor of *Tribuna* literary magazine and director of Editura Dacia publishing house, both of which are based in the city of Cluj, Transylvania.

Căpusan, Maria Vodă (1940–2017)   Theatre critic and theorist. Her works include *Teatru şi mit* (*Theatre and Myth*) (1976), *Despre Caragiale* (*On Caragiale*) (1982), *Pragmatica teatrului* (*The Pragmatics of Theatre*) (1987), *Marin Sorescu sau Despre Tînjirea spre cer* (*Marin Sorescu or On the Yearning for Heaven*) (1993), and *Caragiale?* (2002).

Caragiale, Ion Luca (1852–1912)   Writer, playwright, and director of Bucharest's National Theatre. Caragiale was an incisive satirist of Romanian social and political mores. Both in his lifetime and afterwards, Caragiale's work has earned high praise, but also furious opposition on the part of those indignant at his unsparing satirical portrayal of national flaws and weaknesses. His stage comedies, which include *O noapte furtunoasă* (*A Stormy Night*) (1879) and *O scrisoare pierdută* (*A Lost Letter*) (1884), are still a mainstay of the Romanian theatre, satirising, as topically as ever, political corruption, venality, hypocrisy and immorality in public office, tub-thumping jingoism, mawkish patriotic sentiment, favouritism and nepotism, demagogy, the vulgarity and unscrupulous ambition of the parvenu, and petty backstabbing.

Ceuca, Justin (1939–)   Poet and theatre critic. From 1965 to 1995 he was the Literary Director of the National Theatre, Cluj. His works include *Melancolii* (*Melancholias*) (1987), *Teatrologia românească interbelică* (*Inter-war Romanian Theatrology*) (1990), and *Evoluţia formelor dramatice* (*The Evolution of Dramatic Forms*) (2002).

Cioabă, Mirela (1955–)   Actress and teacher at the University of Craiova. She appeared in *The Death of Mr Lăzărescu* (2005), directed by Cristi Puiu, a major film of the Romanian New Wave.

Ciulei, Liviu (1923–2011)   Film and theatre director, actor, costume and set designer, and architect, Ciulei was a true Renaissance man, a towering figure of Romanian and world theatre. He studied at the Royal Conservatory of Music and Theatre, Bucharest, graduating in 1946, and then at the Ion Mincu School of Architecture, graduating in 1949. He made his debut as an actor in the role of Puck in a production of *A Midsummer Night's Dream* staged at the Odeon, Bucharest, in 1946, before joining the company of the Municipal Theatre (later to be renamed the Bulandra, q.v.), where he directed his first stage production in 1957. In 1965, he won the Directors' Award at Cannes for his screen adaptation of Liviu Rebreanu's novel *The Forest of the Hanged*, in which he also had an acting part. From 1963 to 1974, he was theatre manager at the Bulandra, staging dazzling productions of a string of classics that included *As You Like It*, *Macbeth*, *The Tempest*, *The Lower Depths*, *Danton's Death*, *The Threepenny Opera*, *A Streetcar Named Desire*, and *Long Day's Journey Into Night*. He was sacked from the Bulandra by the communist authorities as a result of the scandal surrounding Lucian Pintilie's (q.v.) subversive production of Gogol's *The Government Inspector*, which was banned after only three performances. In the 1970s, he was invited to direct plays at major theatres around the world, winning the Australian Critics' Award in 1977 for his production of Gorki's *The Lower Depths* in Sydney. In 1980, Ciulei left Romania permanently, and from 1980 to 1985, he was the artistic director of the Guthrie Theatre, Minneapolis, where he directed *The Tempest*, *As You Like It*, *Twelfth Night*, *A Midsummer Night's Dream*, *Peer Gynt*, *The Threepenny Opera*, and *Three Sisters*, among other plays. From 1986 to 1990, he taught Theatre Direction at Columbia University. Returning to Romania after the 1989 Revolution, he continued to direct theatre to great acclaim, and was named Honorary Director of the Bulandra, the theatre to which he had dedicated so much of his career as an actor, director, and set designer, and to the rebuilding of which he had contributed as an architect.

Ciupe, T. Th. (1933–2010)   Leading Romanian set designer. T. Th. Ciupei studied stage design at the Nicolae Grigorescu Institute of Plastic Arts, graduating in 1958, and went on to work at the National Theatre in Cluj. He worked with numerous important directors, including Aureliu Manea. He won awards for the sets he designed for *As You Like It*, directed by Alexandru Dabija in 1979, and *Hamlet*, directed by Gábor Trompa in 1996.

Cocora, Ion (1938–)   Poet and theatre critic, manager of the Theatrum Mundi, Bucharest, director of the Palimpsest publishing house, member of the International Association of Theatre Critics. His collections of poems include *Palimpsest* (1969), *Suverenitate lăuntrică* (*Inner Sovereignty*) (1975), and *Plante de dincolo* (*Plants From the Other Side*) (1983). Cocora was a close friend of Aureliu Manea, and encouraged him to express his ideas about the theatre in writing, leading to the publication of *Imaginary Performances. Confessions.*

Cubleşan, Constantin (1939–)   Novelist, playwright, poet, literary critic, and historian. He studied Russian at the Victor Babeş University, Cluj, graduating in 1959. In 1982, he was awarded a doctorate for his thesis on the work of playwright Barbu Ştefănescu-Delavrancea (q.v.). He was manager of the National Theatre, Cluj, from 1980 to 1987.

Ichim, Florica (1945–) Film and theatre critic. Since 1997, she has been editor-in-chief of *Teatrul azi* (*Theatre Today*), Romania's leading theatre review.

Ieremia, Ioan (1935–) During the communist period, Ieremia worked as a director at the National Theatre, Timişoara, and Teatrul Mic (The Little Theatre), Bucharest. In 1977, he was sacked from Teatrul Mic after signing Charta 77. In 1987, he was sacked from the National Theatre, Timişoara, for "anti-Party and anti-State performances."

Liiceanu, Gabriel (1942–) Romanian philosopher and head of Humanitas, now Romania's leading publisher, founded in 1990 after the fall of the communist regime. His works include *Tragicul. O fenomenologie a limitei şi depăşirii* (*The Tragic. A Phenomenology of the Limit and Transgression*) (1975), *Jurnalul de la Păltiniş* (*Păltiniş Diary*) (1983, an account of philosopher Constantin Noica (1909–1987), who was imprisoned during the Stalinist period, and of resistance through culture in a totalitarian society), *Uşa interzisă* (*The Forbidden Door*) (2002), *Despre minciună* (*On Lying*) (2006), *Despre ură* (*On Hatred*) (2007), and *Aşteptînd o altă omenire* (*Awaiting a Different Humankind*) (2018).

Mazilu, Teodor (1930–1980) Actor, playwright, prose writer. His highly popular plays ridiculed the absurdities of totalitarian Romania. *Proştii sub clar de lună* (*Morons in the Moonlight*), directed by Lucian Pintilie (q.v.) at the Bulandra Theatre (q.v.) in 1963 during the Gheorghiu-Dej period, prior to the partial cultural "thaw" brought by the first few years of the Ceauşescu regime in the late 1960s, was banned by the authorities. His other plays include *Aceşti nebuni făţarnici* (*These Sanctimonious Fools*) (1971) and *Mobilă şi durere* (*Furniture and Pain*) (1980). In 1972, he published a philosophical essay titled *Ipocrizia disperării* (*The Hypocrisy of Despair*).

Micu, Dan (1949–1999) Romanian theatre director. He directed productions at the National Theatre, Notarra, and Bulandra (q.v.) in Bucharest. After 1989, he was general manager of Teatrul Mic (The Little Theatre) until his premature death in 1999. His productions included *The Cold* by Marin Sorescu (q.v.), *The Gnome in the Summer Garden* by D. R. Popescu (q.v.), *A Stormy Night* by Ion Luca Caragiale (q.v.), and *The Karamazovs*, an adaptation of the Dostoevsky novel.

Muşatescu, Tudor (1903–1970) Playwright, director, humourist. His plays include *Titanic-Vals* (*Titanic Waltz*) (1932), . . . *escu* (1933), *Visul unei nopţi de iarnă* (*A Midwinter Night's Dream*) (1937), and *A murit Bubi* (*Bubi Is Dead*) (1948). In *Titanic Waltz*, an unassuming functionary working in the mayor's office of a provincial town is pushed by his family into standing for parliament and is elected when voters are swayed by the frankness of his admission that he will not be able to do anything for them. The big-screen adaptation of *Titanic Waltz* (1965, 95 min.), directed by Paul Călinescu and starring Grigore Vasiliu-Birlic (1905–1970), is one of the most popular Romanian film comedies of all time.

Penciulescu, Radu (1930–2019)   Leading Romanian director and devotee of the Stanislavski method. From 1964 to 1969, he was manager of Teatrul Mic (the Little Theatre), Bucharest, at the same time teaching at the Institute of Theatrical and Cinematographic Arts. In 1973, he emigrated to Sweden, where he taught acting at the Malmö Theatre Institute. After the 1989 Revolution, he returned to Romania to direct productions of plays by Shakespeare at the National Theatre, Bucharest.

Petrescu, Irina (1941–2013)   Film and theatre actress. She studied at the Ion Luca Caragiale Institute of Theatrical and Cinematographic Arts, graduating in 1963. Her numerous roles included Lena in Liviu Ciulei's (q.v.) production of Büchner's *Leonce and Lena* at the Bulandra (q.v.) in 1970; Ines in Mihai Mănuțiu's production of Sartre's *Huis Clos* at the Bulandra in 1982; Margot in Cătălina Buzoianu's (q.v.) production of Gabriela Adameșteanu's *A Wasted Morning* at the Bulandra in 1986; Célimène in Valeriu Moisescu's production of Molière's *The Misanthrope* at the Bulandra in 1989; Maria Vasilyevna Voynitskaya in Yuriy Kordonskiy's production of Chekhov's *Uncle Vanya* at the Bulandra in 2001; and Nell in Alexandru Tocilescu's (q.v.) production of Samuel Beckett's *Endgame* at the Metropolis in 2009. She also starred in numerous feature films, including *A Woman for a Season* (1969), for which she won the award for Best Actress at the Sixth Moscow International Film Festival.

Pintilie, Lucian (1933–2018)   Theatre and film director, screenwriter. From 1960 to 1972 he was a resident director at the Bulandra Theatre (q.v.), Bucharest, where his productions included Teodor Mazilu's (q.v.) *Morons in the Moonlight* (1962), Ion Luca Caragiale's (q.v.) *Carnival Scenes* (1966), Chekhov's *The Cherry Orchard* (1967), and Gogol's *The Government Inspector* (1974), which was banned by the authorities after its third performance. During the same period, he directed two feature films: *Sunday at Six* (1966), a psychological drama, and *The Reconstruction* (1968). Based on a true story, the second of these films narrates the police reconstruction of a brawl between two youths, which culminates in an actual killing. The film outraged the communist authorities and dictator Nicolae Ceaușescu personally ordered that it be banned. *The Reconstruction* has been named the best Romanian film of all time by the Association of Romanian Film Critics. After the banning of his production of *The Government Inspector*, Pintilie managed to leave Romania and continued to direct theatre in France and the

United States. At the Théâtre de la Ville, Paris, he directed productions of *The Seagull* (1975), *Three Sisters* (1979), *The Wild Duck* (1981), and *The Lower Depths* (1983), among others. At the Guthrie Theater, Minneapolis, he directed *The Seagull* (1983), *Tartuffe* (1984), and *The Wild Duck* (1988). Returning to Romania in 1990 after the Revolution, he completed a series of films previously left unfinished because of communist censorship. In 1998, he won the Jury Prize at the Venice Film Festival for *Terminus Paradis*, a French-Romanian co-production.

Popescu, D. R. (1935–) Novelist, playwright, screenwriter, and member of the Romanian Academy. His novels have been described as being in a vein similar to South American magic realism. A prolific playwright, his major achievements are *Aceşti îngeri trişti* (*These Sad Angels*) (1969), *Piticul din grădina de vară* (*The Gnome in the Summer Garden*) (1973), and *Pasărea Shakespeare* (*The Shakespeare Bird*) (1973).

Preda, Gheorghe (1960–) Film director and screenwriter. Preda has written and directed the feature films *The Song of Songs* (1993), *Paradise Regained* (1996), *The Necessary Angel* (2007), *The Finnish Cow* (2012), *Camera Obscura* (2016), and *The Erotic Pharmacy* (2018). In 2010, he directed a short film based on a screenplay by Aureliu Manea, titled *The Breakdown*.

Prelipceanu, Nicolae (1942–) Poet, prose writer, and journalist. Prelipceanu is editor-in-chief of *Viaţa Românească* (*Romanian Life*). He has published numerous collections of poetry, including *Turnul inclinat* (*Leaning Tower*) (1966) and *Jurnal de noapte* (*Night Diary*) (1980), and prose, including *Zece minute de nemurire* (*Ten Minutes of Immortality*) (1983) and *Scara interioară* (*The Inner Stairs*) (1987). He was a very close friend of Aureliu Manea.

Raicu, Lucian (1934–2006) Major literary critic. He emigrated to Paris in 1986. His works include *Structuri literare* (*Literary Structures*) (1974), *Gogol sau fantastical banalităţii* (*Gogol or the Fantasticality of the Banal*) (1974), *Critica—forma de viaţă* (*Criticism—Form of Life*) (1976), and *Scene din romanul literaturii* (*Scenes From the Novel of Literature*) (1985).

România Literară Literary and cultural magazine. A short-lived magazine of this title was published in Jassy by poet Vasile Alexsandri over the course of eleven months in 1855 until it was banned by the authorities. The title was revived in 1968 for a weekly magazine based in Bucharest. *România Literară* (*Literary Romania*) is the official publication of the Union of Romanian Writers.

Salzberger, Paul (1945–) Set designer. Paul Salzberger has designed more than sixty theatre productions in Romania and Israel. He worked extensively with Aureliu Manea and was one of his closest friends.

Scarlat, Nicolae (1940–)   Director and theatre manager. His many productions include plays by Matei Vişniec, Barbu Ştefănescu Delavrancea (q.v.), D. R. Popescu (q.v.), Ion Luca Caragiale (q.v.), Teodor Mazilu (q.v.), Tudor Muşatescu (q.v.), William Shakespeare, Molière, Dario Fo, Georg Büchner, and Johan Strindberg.

Silvestru, Valentin (1924–1996)   Theatre critic, playwright, prose writer, and journalist. Silvestru (pen name of Marcel Moscovici) was best known for his short sketches, as collected in *Glastra cu sfecle* (*The Beetroot Flowerpot*) (1965), for example, in which he finds humour in the absurdities of everyday life in communist Romania, with its characteristic speech patterns, pointless bureaucracy and petty bribery, nepotism, low-level imposture, socialist social-climbing, and specific styles of boorishness.

Sorescu, Marin (1936–1996)   A major post-war Romanian poet, Sorescu has been translated in every major European language. He was also an important playwright: his *Thirst of the Salt Mountain* (1974) trilogy of plays, comprising *Jonah, The Sexton,* and *The Riverbed,* is a highly original and radical experiment in absurdist theatre. Given the extraordinary acting and technical challenges it presents, *Jonah* was not staged until 1991, in a production directed by Ioan Ieremia (q.v.) at the National Theatre Bucharest.

Ştefănescu-Delavrancea, Barbu (1858–1918)   Writer, playwright, poet, lawyer, orator, and politician. His plays include the *Moldavia Trilogy: Sunset* (1909), *The Blizzard* (1910), *The Evening Star* (1910), and *Hadji Tudose* (1912).

Tocilescu (Toca), Alexandru (1946–2011)   Theatre and film director. Tocilescu directed plays and operas by Johan Strindberg, Eugene O'Neill, William Shakespeare, Stephen Poliakoff, Sophocles, Mikhail Bulgakov, Gounod, Ion Luca Caragiale (q.v.), and Samuel Beckett at theatres in Bucharest (Teatrul Mic, the Bulandra (q.v.), the National Theatre, the Metropolis, Theatrum Mundi) and Satu Mare, Brăila, Piteşti, Piatra Neamţ, Braşov, and Constanţa.

Visarion, Alexa (1947–)   Leading theatre and film director, playwright, and screenwriter. He has directed over one hundred plays both in Romania and abroad, including works by Chekhov, Shakespeare, and O'Neill, and seven feature films, including *Năpasta* (*The Calamity*) (1982), a screen adaptation of Ion Luca Caragiale's (q.v.) only non-comic play; *Vinovatul* (*The Guilty Party*) (1991); *Luna Verde* (*Green Moon*) (2008); and *Ana* (2014). In the 1980s, he was the recipient of two Fulbright grants, and taught filmmaking as a visiting professor at universities in Dallas, Los Angeles, New York, and Boston.

Zărnescu, Constantin (1949–)   Novelist and playwright. His plays include *Regina Iocasta* (*Queen Jocasta*) (1981).

Zitta, Vali (1948–2010)   Romanian-Hungarian actress.

Index

Note: Page numbers in *italics* indicate a figure on the corresponding page.

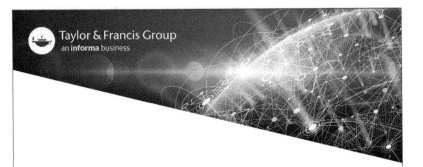